19th July
25'
13'

D1375777

4 1 0041017 6

CHOOSE LIFE

CHRISTMAS AND EASTER SERMONS IN CANTERBURY CATHEDRAL

ARCHBISHOP ROWAN WILLIAMS

BLOOMSBURY

LONDON • NEW DELHI • NEW YORK • SYDNEY

First published in Great Britain 2013

Copyright © Rowan Williams, 2013

The moral right of the author has been asserted

No part of this book may be used or reproduced in any manner
whatsoever without written permission from the Publisher except in
the case of brief quotations embodied in critical articles or reviews.
Every reasonable effort has been made to trace copyright holders of
material reproduced in this book, but if any have been inadvertently
overlooked the Publishers would be glad to hear from them.

A Continuum book

Bloomsbury Publishing Plc
50 Bedford Square
London WC1B 3DP

www.bloomsbury.com

Bloomsbury Publishing, London, New Delhi, New York and Sydney

A CIP record for this book is available from the British Library.

ISBN 9781408190388

10 9 8 7 6 5 4 3 2 1

Typeset by Fakenham Prepress Solutions, Fakenham, Norfolk
NR21 8NN

Printed and bound in Great Britain by CPI Group (UK) Ltd,
Croydon CR0 4YY

MIX
Paper from
responsible sources
FSC
www.fsc.org
FSC® C020471

CONTENTS

Preface
ix

CHRISTMAS SERMONS

The Kingdom of the Simple
3

'Fear Not!'
13

'From His Fullness We Have All Received'
23

The Life Story of God
31

The Poorest Deserve the Best
39

The Marriage of Heaven and Earth
49

Global Saviours, Mortal Messiahs
59

Contents

The Heir of All Creation
69

Great is Thy Faithfulness
79

The Word of Life, the Words of Prayer
89

Stopping and Seeing
99

EASTER SERMONS

Letting Go
111

Into Daylight
121

Presente
127

The Denial of Death
135

Conspiracies and Transparencies
143

Liberating Truth
153

Swallowed Up in Victory
161

The Hidden Seed of Glory
171

Showing Signs of Life
181

Happiness or Joy?
191

But is it True?
201

PREFACE

Easter and Christmas are the defining points of the year for all Christians. Easter marks the event that changes the entire landscape of how we talk about, and think about, and relate to both God and humanity; Christmas celebrates that mysterious and unique coming-together of God and humanity which makes Easter itself possible. The whole of Christian doctrine and devotion unfolds from these two celebrations, from the resurrection of Jesus and the birth of the eternal Word of God in flesh and blood.

So these are festivals that pose a challenge to any preacher. We are familiar with the stories and the doctrines; but how can you begin either to speak adequately of events on which the whole history of humankind turns, or to speak freshly of events that have exercised the best gifts of mind and imagination among Christians for two millennia? And because you're likely on these occasions to be preaching to a somewhat wider audience than committed Christians alone, how do you begin to make the connections between these world-altering mysteries and the questions and crises of contemporary public life and human experience?

These sermons are in part an attempt to build a few bridges between these different worlds of understanding. But they are not meant as current affairs commentary with a bit of religious colouring. I have tried, with whatever uneven degree of success, never to lose sight of the fact that what we celebrate in our festivals is the action of the living God in and through the particular humanity of Jesus of Nazareth as recorded in Scripture and reflected in the creeds. To be personal: I have found throughout my ministry that the shape of Christian doctrine as set out in these creeds is an inexhaustible resource in making sense of the complexities of human experience, of politics and economics and the often tormented psychology of men and women. 'Orthodoxy' is not therefore another word for mechanical traditionalism. It means for me and countless others a wellspring of insight and delight. I can only pray that these meditations may at least help to prompt a suspicion that the story which takes shape around the birth and resurrection of Jesus may after all be the story upon which all the diversity of human exploration and journeying converges.

Rowan Williams
Lambeth Palace, All Saints, 2012

A note on the Lectionary

With two exceptions the Archbishop's sermons gathered here were all given at the main morning celebration of the Eucharist at Christmas or Easter, at which, following the Church of England's *Common Worship* lectionary, the scriptural readings were:

Christmas	**Easter**
Isaiah 52.7–10	*Isaiah* 65.17–end
Psalm 98	*or Acts* 10.34–43
Hebrews 1.1–12	*Psalm* 118.1–2, 14–24
John 1.1–14	*1 Corinthians* 15.19–26
	or Acts 10.34–43
	John 20.1–18

(The reading from Acts must be used as either the first or second reading.)

Christmas Sermons

THE KINGDOM OF THE SIMPLE

Christmas Day broadcast 2002

> The low vault was full of lamps and the
> air close and still. Silver bells announced
> the coming of the three bearded, vested
> monks, who like the kings of old now
> prostrated themselves before the altar. So
> the long liturgy began.
>
> Helena knew little Greek and her
> thoughts were not in the words nor
> anywhere near the immediate scene. She
> forgot everything except the swaddled
> child long ago and those three royal sages
> who had come from so far to adore him.
>
> 'This is my day', she thought, 'and these
> are my kind.'

Helena is speaking some seventeen hundred
years ago; she is the Empress Helena, mother
of Constantine the Great in Evelyn Waugh's
1950 novel named for her. Late in life, she has
discovered the new faith of Christianity, and sets

off to the Holy Land to anchor her new belief in
the sheer physical facts of history and geography
– because what is different about Christianity is
that it identifies the mystery of God with a set
of prosaic happenings in a specific place. God
is just there for all, not locked up in technical
language or mystical speculation, but, as Helena
has said earlier in the novel, the answer to a
child's questions: When? Where? How do you
know?

But Helena, longing for this simple vision, is still
caught up in the bitter, devious world of politics.
Her son the Emperor, confused and anxious at
his own extraordinary success in subduing the
Roman World, gets more and more embroiled
in palace intrigue, in espionage and assassina-
tions, in black magic, in the hall of mirrors that
is the daily life of the powerful. Helena, brisk
and honest though she is, can't completely avoid
getting caught up in this too; feeling trapped in
Constantine's world of plots and fantastic visions
of a new world order, she sets off for Jerusalem to
find the remains of the cross of Jesus.

So here she is in church at Bethlehem, tired and
puzzled. And suddenly, as the priests process

solemnly to begin the service, the story of the three wise men makes sense to her of some of what she's experienced. These so-called wise men were her sort of people, the people she was used to: clever, devious, complicated, nervous; the late arrivals on the scene.

'Like me', she said to them, 'you were late in coming. The shepherds were here long before; even the cattle. They had joined the chorus of angels before you were on your way …

'How laboriously you came, taking sights and calculating, where the shepherds had run barefoot! How odd you looked on the road, attended by what outlandish liveries, laden with such preposterous gifts!

'You came at length to the final stage of your pilgrimage and the great star stood still above you. What did you do? You stopped to call on King Herod. Deadly exchange of compliments in which began that unended war of mobs and magistrates against the innocent!'

Even on their way to Christ, the wise men create the typical havoc that complicated people create; telling Herod about the Christ child, they provoke the massacre of the children in Bethlehem. It's as if, in Helena's eyes, the wise, the devious and resourceful can't help making the most immense mistakes of all. The strategists, who know all the possible ramifications of politics, miss the huge and obvious things and create yet more havoc and suffering. After all, centuries after Helena, here we still are, tangled in the same net, knowing more and more, stepping deeper and deeper into tragedy. Communications are more effective than ever in human history; analysis of national and international situations becomes ever more subtle; intelligence and surveillance provide more and more material. We have endless theoretical perspectives on human behaviour, individual and collective. And still the innocent are killed.

Yet – here is the miracle – the three wise men are welcome. You might expect that a faith which begins in such blinding simplicities, the child, the cattle, the barefoot shepherds, would have no place for the wise men in their massive foolishness. But, thinks Helena ...

'You came and were not turned away.
You too found room before the manger.
Your gifts were not needed, but they
were accepted and put carefully by, for
they were brought with love. In that new
order of charity that had just come to life,
there was room for you too.'

Coming to the Christ child isn't always simple. It just is the case that people come by roundabout routes, with complex histories, sin and muddle and false perceptions and wrong starts. It's no good saying to them, 'You must become simple and wholehearted', as if this could be done just by wishing it. The real question is, 'Can you take all your complicated history with you on a journey towards the manger? Can you at least refuse to settle down in the hall of mirrors, and go on asking where truth really lies? Can you stop hanging on to the complex and the devious for their own sake, as a theatre for your skills, and recognize where the map of the heavens points?'

'You are my especial patrons,' said
Helena, 'and patrons of all late-comers,
of all who have a tedious journey to make
to the truth, of all who are confused

with knowledge and speculation, of all
who through politeness make themselves
partners in guilt, of all who stand in
danger by reason of their talents.

'Dear cousins, pray for me,' said Helena,
'and for my poor overloaded son. May
he, too, before the end find kneeling
space in the straw. Pray for the great, lest
they perish utterly.'

So: don't deny the tangle and the talents, the
varied web of what has made you who you are.
Every step is part of the journey; on this journey,
even the false starts are part of the journey,
experience that moves you on towards truth. It
won't do to think of Christianity as a faith that
demands of you an embarrassed pretence of a
simplicity that has no connection with reality;
isn't this what so often leads people not to take
Christianity seriously? As though you had to leave
the full range of human experience outside the
door (the stable door), while the innocent alone
entered without challenge?

Helena's answer is worth pondering. Bring what
has made you who you are and bring it, neither in

pride nor in embarrassment, but in order to offer it as a gift. It's possible to say to God, 'Use what my experience and my mistakes and false starts have made me in order to let your transfiguring love show through.' It's true that the Christmas event is precisely the answer to the simplest of human questions, to the 'When? Where? How do you know?' demands of the child. It's true that those who are least well defended by sophistication and self-reflection get there first. They have fewer deceptions to shed, fewer ways of holding God at arm's length, while so many of us have a lifetime's expertise in this. From them we learn where to look; we know how much we long for that sheer presence and accessibility of God, the bare fact of the child in the manger, the life in Galilee, the mystery laid open. But we come as we are; room is made for us, healing is promised for us, even usefulness given to us if we are ready to make an offering of what W. H. Auden called our crooked heart. Evelyn Waugh knew something about this himself – like so many writers, he knew what it was for imagination to twist round on itself like a snake, he knew about the gaps that open between work and life, how a work finished and beautiful in its own terms emerges out of a human background of failure and confusion. He had no illusions about himself, recognizing the melancholy, anger and hyper-sensitivity that shadowed his life. His Helena is praying for her literary creator; the writing is a prayer for absolution.

In the straw of the stable, the humble and the complicated are able to kneel together. If God is there in the simplicity of the baby in the straw, the answer to a child's question, that means he is there in naked simplicity for the sophisticated and troubled as well, those who have had long and tortuous journeys, cold comings, to the stable. Yes, we are told to become like children, faced with the invitation to believe and trust in the God of Bethlehem. But that is not the same as saying, as we all too often do, 'Christmas is a time for the children', meaning that it has nothing to say to grown-ups, who indulge the pretty fantasy for a short while but stay firmly outside the stable door.

Helena knows better. The childlike response of longing and delight can come even from a heart that has grown old and tired; and when such a response arises, let no-one think that they are too compromised, too entangled to be welcome.

Waugh's novel depicts a whole world grown old in intrigue and violence, cynicism, despair and false hope, and says that there is true hope in spite of all, in the indestructible fact of a cradle and a bit of stained old timber that once carried a human body in its death agonies, the cross that Helena finds in Jerusalem. Space has been made in this world, the real world of politics and struggle, for God to make himself at home, and to welcome all of us and use whatever we bring him.

So Helena prays for the late-comers, the confused, the gifted, the powerful who have so little power and freedom, the civilized and sensible who find, too late, that they have stood by and endorsed cruelty or corruption, those who have grown old and used to cynicism. The wise men stand at the cradle with a clear job to do for us, and Helena addresses them, unforgettably:

> 'For His sake who did not reject your
> curious gifts, pray always for all the
> learned, the oblique, the delicate. Let
> them not be quite forgotten at the
> Throne of God when the simple come
> into their kingdom.'

'FEAR NOT!'

Christmas 2003

'Fear not!', says the angel to Joseph, to Mary, to the shepherds. It is a recurring motif in the Christmas stories, and a significant reminder that the overwhelming news of God the Saviour's coming is both all that the human heart could hope for and also something that powerfully disrupts the way the world goes and the way our lives go. There is something to be afraid of in the renewal of a world: I may not welcome being reconstructed or interrupted.

Religious commitment of any depth is bound to say to the world around it that the assumptions and habits of that world are not beyond question. It isn't all that surprising if a secular environment looks at religion not only with suspicion or incomprehension but with fear. The proposal to ban Muslim headscarves in French schools suggests that there is still a nervousness about letting commitment show its face in public, lest ground be given to some threatening irrational power that will take over the world of reasonable people. President Chirac himself has defended the proposal by claiming that a school must be a 'republican sanctuary' in which children are protected from the cold winds of sectarianism while they absorb the proper values of their society. Religious belief is not banned, but its outward expression – the crucifix on the wall as much as the headscarf – has to be strictly controlled so that the purity of the nation's values may be preserved. Faith must be invisible.

And at the same time, the Chief Rabbi of France encourages the men of his congregations to avoid wearing the skull cap in public because of the spiralling of anti-Semitic incidents. There's more than one reason for religious commitment to be made invisible; sometimes invisibility is sought. Here, then, are two quite different aspects of the public face of religious belief and the complex reactions and feelings it produces – a secular world determined to protect itself against any show of religious faith; a religious community fearful about proclaiming its identity in public because of hatred towards its members. Different problems, different motivations; but behind both lies one central and urgent challenge to do with the public face of religious belief in the modern world.

For all our talk about pluralism, many still feel in all kinds of ways uncomfortable when religion makes a visible difference in public life – so that in turn religious people may feel excluded or threatened if they are visibly identified as members of a community of faith. Discomfort about religion, or about a particular religion, may be the response of an educated liberal or, at the opposite extreme, the unthinking violence of an anti-Semite; it isn't easy to face the fact that sometimes the effects are similar for the believer. And in case we think the whole debate is just a French problem, we should recognize just a little of the same unease in the nervous sniggering about the Prime Minister's religious faith which ripples over the surface of the media from time to time, or in the blustering irritation aroused by something like Joanna Jepson's whistleblowing about our assumptions around abortion.

The fear of faith itself is part of what can breed fear in a vulnerable or minority community, of whatever tradition. And before we rise up and angrily deplore this, it's worth pausing to ask just why faith provokes such a passionate protectiveness. Historically, the answer is, alas, that religious faith has too often been the language of

15

the powerful, the excuse for oppression, the alibi for atrocity. It has appeared as itself intolerant of difference (hence the legacy of anti-Semitism), as a campaigning, aggressive force for uniformity, as a self-defensive and often corrupt set of institutions indifferent to basic human welfare. That's a legacy that dies hard, however much we might want to protest that it is far from the whole picture. And it's given new life by the threat of terror carried out in the name of a religion – even when representatives of that religion at every level roundly condemn such action as incompatible with faith.

The believer says to the secular world, 'Don't be afraid!' Yet religion has appeared as something fighting to take over territory in the human soul and the human world – an empire pushing at the frontiers, struggling to defeat the independence and dignity of people. You may remember Swinburne's famous lines – 'Thou hast conquered, O pale Galilean! The world has grown grey with thy breath.' That sums up what a great many people at least half believe. It comes from a highly selective version of history, yet it has enough plausibility to need an answer at the very deepest level.

And this is what our Christmas story and our Christmas faith offer. Why should Joseph and Mary and the shepherds not be afraid? Because what happens when God comes to earth is not something like the first landing of an occupying army, the first breach in our defences by a powerful enemy who wants to take all that is ours. The truth is as different as could be; and the clue is in those simple words, simple words that invite a lifetime's joyful reflection: 'The Word was made flesh'.

When God comes among us, he doesn't first of all clear humanity out of the way so that he can take over; he becomes a human being. He doesn't force his way in to dominate and crush; he announces his arrival in the sharp, hungry cry of a newborn baby. He changes the world not by law and threat but by death and resurrection. Robert Southwell's poem wonderfully captures this overturning of all our terrors and apprehensions:

> His batt'ring shots are babish cries,
> His arrows looks of weeping eyes.

And the anonymous mediaeval lyric puts it unforgettably:

17

He came al so stille, Where his mother was,
As dew in Aprille, That falleth on the grass.

He comes in stillness. He comes in dependency
and weakness. He comes by God's absolutely
free gift. Yet he comes from the heart of our
own human world and life, from the womb of a
mother, from the free love of Mary's heart given
to God in trust. And this is mysteriously the same
thing as his 'coming down from heaven'. He
is utterly different, the human being who lives
God's own life; he is utterly the same, like us in
all things, as the Bible says.

The manner of his coming tells us so many things –
but not the least is that human nature, bruised and
disfigured as it is by sin, is still capable of bearing
the life of God. In the birth of God in flesh and
blood, we see what we were made to be – carriers
of divine love. And with this birth we begin our
journey back to where we belong, back to God,
back to what we were made to be. To live in peace
and delight with God does not mean that our
humanity has first to undergo such radical surgery
that it barely seems human any more, that our
nature has to be beaten into submission by a divine
aggressor. He came all so still; he came to his own.

Here then is the real Christian response to the modern secular person's fear. God is no hostile alien, snatching away what belongs to us. Faith is not either a perversion of human freedom or a marginal and private eccentricity. It is human freedom raised to its fullest by the fact that God has embraced it in love – 'from his fullness have we all received, grace upon grace'. The Word, as St John makes plain in this morning's gospel, is no stranger in the world; he is the very centre and energy of creation itself, the heart of every heart.

So Christian faith does not seek to carve out a territory to defend for itself, nor does it look to take over a potentially rebellious world and subdue it by force. It simply witnesses to the world that the world will never be fully itself except in the glad receiving of God's presence and the recognition of the 'true light' at the centre of all human, all created life. If this makes us afraid, the Christian will say, that is because at some level we are afraid of ourselves, of what we really are and might be; afraid of a destiny for human beings more glorious than we could imagine; afraid that we may have to change our lives unrecognizably in order truly to become ourselves.

No, it isn't comfortable: it may be terrifying. 'He came to his own', yes, 'and his own would not receive him' – and 'his own' in this context is all of us who are made in his image and who yet can't cope with his promise. And because we people of faith have so often behaved as though we had never heard or understood the Christmas gospel, we can't expect the secular world to believe us straight away when we say that they have nothing to worry about and that faith is the flowering of human dignity not its opposite. First we have to show that we truly are on the side of humanity – by patient loyalty to people in their need, by courage and sacrifice for the sake of justice, by labour for reconciliation, setting people free from the threat of violence. God comes to 'his own people', religious people, and we have often failed to know or receive him.

And then, supposing we have cleared away the fears that arise from the way religious people have failed to witness fully to their God – then the deeper fears can and do come to the surface, the fears of what faith may demand of a person. Nothing will take away the challenge here; we can only hope that there are enough lives showing joy and humanity to make the challenge worthwhile

– lives in which the eternal Word will speak. Such lives will have about them the great mark of God's action in Jesus, which is that he doesn't invade, doesn't push us out of the way, doesn't reduce or demean us; he invites, he opens up to us his own infinite hospitality, drawing us into his world, his life. He makes us more than we are, not less. And that is what the true person of faith will show in their life. When the life of faith is visible in the public world, it is not something threatening the integrity of the supposedly neutral and obvious moral principles of the secular state; it is a glimpse into the depths of all morality, all principle and commitment, into the depths where the holiness and faithfulness and love of God secretly nourish the essence of human life, that life which is made for the destiny of becoming children of God. It is a glimpse into a richness surrounding all that we are, without which all our vaunted values and principles would soon corrupt and die.

All our great religious traditions say something of this – which is one reason for Christians, Muslims, Jews and others to stand with each other and speak out for each other in times of stress or harassment. Yet the uniqueness of our Christian faith is that it is inscribed for us not only in a text, but in a living human presence in which dwells all the fullness of God. We may confidently say to a nervous secular world, 'Fear not!' God is not coming to abolish but to fulfil the hopes of liberty and human dignity. But we ourselves as believers need to hear the same words we speak to others: 'Fear not!' We don't have to fight for our claims in such a way that all the world sees is another power-obsessed and anxious human institution; we have only to let the Word be born in us and speak in us. A lifetime's work, but also a moment's gift, in the sudden grasp of the mystery of this celebration of God made human, in the words we hear from the gospel, in the bread and wine of the Eucharist: 'from his fullness we have all received, grace upon grace.'

'From His Fullness We Have All Received'

Christmas 2004

It used to be said that if you were travelling by ocean liner, the worst thing you could do was to visit the engine room; and I'm afraid it's a point people make to discourage you from visiting the Vatican, or Church House, or even Lambeth Palace. Getting too close to the centre of things – or at least what people *think* is the centre of things – can be alarming or disillusioning or both: you really don't want to know that, people will say; you don't need to know how things work (or fail to work). Get on with it.

And that's where Christmas is actually a bit strange and potentially worrying. When we're invited into the stable to see the child, it's really being invited into the engine room. This is how God works; this is how God is. The entire system of the universe, 'the fire in the equations' as someone wonderfully described it,[1] is contained in this small bundle of shivering flesh. God has given himself away so completely that we meet him here in poverty and weakness, with no trumpeting splendour, no clouds of glory. This is how he is: he acts by giving away all we might expect to find in him of strength and success as we understand them. The universe lives by a love that refuses to bully us or force us, the love of the cradle and the cross.

It ought to shock us to be told year after year that the universe lives by the kind of love that we see in the helpless child and in the dying man on the cross. We have been shown the engine room of the universe; and it ought to worry us – us, who are so obsessed about being safe and being successful, who worry endlessly about being in control, who cannot believe that power could show itself in any other way than the ways we are used to. But this festival tells us exactly what Good Friday and Easter tell us: that God fulfils what he wants to do by emptying himself of his own life, giving away all that he is in love. The gospel reading sets this out in terms that cannot be argued with or surpassed. God is always, from all eternity, pouring out his very being in the person of the Word, the everlasting Son; and the Word, who has received everything from the gift of the Father, and who makes the world alive by giving reality to all creation, makes a gift of himself by becoming human and suffering humiliation and death for our sake. 'From his fullness we have all received.' Jesus, the word made human flesh and blood, has given us the freedom, the authority, to become God's children by our trust in him, and so to have a fuller and fuller share in God's own joy.

We live from him and in him. The whole universe exists because God has not held back his love but allowed it to flow without impediment out of his own perfection to make a world that is different from him and then to fill it with love through the gift of his Son. And our life as Christians, our obligations, our morality, do not rest on commands alone, but on the fact that God has given us something of his own life. We are caught up in his giving, in his creative self-sacrifice; true Christian morality is when we can't help ourselves, can't stop ourselves pouring out the kind of love that makes others live. Morality, said one prominent modern Greek Orthodox theologian, is not about right and wrong, it's about reality and unreality, living in Christ or living for yourself. Being good is living in the truth, living a real life, a life that is in touch with 'the fire in the equations' and that lets the intense creativity of God through into his world. The goodness of the Christian is never a matter of achieving a standard, scoring high marks in a test. It is letting the wonder of God's love knock sideways your ordinary habits, so that God comes through – the God who achieves his purpose by reckless gift, by the cradle and the cross.

When St Paul in his second letter to the Church in Corinth insists on the need for generosity towards the poor in the Church at Jerusalem, he appeals, not to an abstract moral principle, but to the fact of God becoming human. 'You know the grace of our Lord Jesus Christ,' he writes, 'that though he was rich yet for your sakes he became poor, so that you through his poverty might become rich' (*2 Corinthians* 8.9). He doesn't argue that we must simply reverse the relations, so that those who were poor become rich and those who were rich become poor, but rather for a situation in which everyone has something to contribute to everyone else, everyone has enough liberty to become a giver of life to others. When material poverty is extreme, it is difficult to have that dignity – though, miraculously, so many poor people have it; the greatest gift we can give to another is to let them give as freely as they can, so that they can supply what we are hungry for. Love is given so that love may be born and given in return. That is the engine of the universe; that is what we see in the helpless child of Bethlehem: God so stripped of what we associate with divinity that we can see the divine nature only as God's act of giving away all that he is.

And if we want to live in the truth, to live in reality, to live by the Spirit who is breathed out from the Father and the Word, this has to be our life. It is not an academic question. In the year ahead, this country takes its place in the chair of the G8 group of nations; and we have already heard from the Chancellor of his aspirations for the UK's role in this context. So far, the attainment of the 'Millennium Development Goals' has not progressed very far or very fast. The likelihood of a reduction by half of people living in abject poverty by the year 2015 is not noticeably greater than it was four years ago. There are plenty of ideas around for instruments that would accelerate the pace – the International Finance Facility, a further push on debt reduction, a regime of incentives to encourage pharmaceutical companies to reduce drug prices and improve distribution systems for needy countries, the development of systematic micro-credit schemes, a new look at agricultural subsidies. The new Africa Commission is at least a beginning to the search for coordinated policies. But despite the vision of some in the political world and beyond, the will to take this forward seems to be in short supply. Some developed nations appear deeply indifferent to the goals agreed. It is all too easy to be more interested in other matters – not least the profound anxieties about security that are at the moment so pervasive, massaged by various forces in our public life in the West.

No-one could or would deny that we face exceptional levels of insecurity and serious problems in relation to an unpredictable and widely diffused network of agencies whose goals are slaughter and disruption. It is not a mistake to be concerned about terror; we have seen enough this last year, in Iraq and Ossetia, of the nauseating and conscienceless brutality that is around. But some of you may remember words used at the end of that worrying and wide-ranging television series in the autumn, *The Power of Nightmare:* 'When a society believes in nothing, the only agenda is fear'. We struggle for a secure world;

so we should. But what if our only passion is to be protected, and we lose sight of what we positively and concretely want for ourselves and one another, what we want for the human family? We are not going to be living in the truth if we have no passion for the liberty of God's children, no share in the generosity of God.

So as we go into this next year in which our country can do so much to advance the vision of the Millennium Goals, the year too in which we celebrate the 20th anniversary of Live Aid, why not make this our central priority as churches and as individual Christians? It is a time to ask ourselves whether we are really living in the truth, motivated by the engine of the universe that is revealed to us in the child of Bethlehem. It may mean risk, it will mean facing the prospect that the prosperity of the developed world can't go on expanding indefinitely; it may mean that we have to look at our security far more in terms of how we make each other safe by guaranteeing justice and liberty for each other. But we shall have recovered a passion, a generous anger about the world's needs, that is our surest long-term answer to issues of security because it looks to a situation in which all are free to give and receive.

29

A few years ago, the churches made a tangible difference in their advocacy for debt relief through the Jubilee 2000 campaign. Can the churches of this country do as much again in the coming year in pressing government and financial institutions towards justice – and in motivating their own members to get involved in voluntary action, advocacy and giving? If the answer is yes, we shall have taken a step towards living in the truth. The law of all being, the fire in the equations which has kindled all life and which burns without restriction in every moment of the life of Jesus from birth to resurrection, will have kindled in us. 'I have come to cast fire upon the earth', said Jesus (*Luke* 12.49). We may well and rightly feel a touch of fear as we look into this 'engine room' – the life so fragile and so indestructible, so joyful and so costly. But this is the life of all things, full of grace and truth, the life of the everlasting Word of God; to those who receive him he will give the right, the liberty, to live with his life, and to kindle on earth the flame of his love.

Note

1   Kitty Ferguson, *The Fire in the Equations: Science, religion and the search for God* (West Conshohocken: Templeton Press, 1994).

THE LIFE STORY OF GOD

Christmas 2005

Exactly 12 months ago, on the last Sunday of December 2004, we were beginning to confront the reality of one of the most terrible natural disasters in living memory, the tsunami in South Asia. It's impossible not to be aware of that anniversary: dates are etched in our minds. Our lives aren't just featureless strips of things going on. We make maps of our lives, we tell stories divided by events where something happened to change things. For those most directly involved, the date of 26 December 2004 marks a brutal interruption – the death or injury of someone, terrible anxiety, bereavement, anger and bewilderment. But for all of us, the date will carry significance, for all of us something erupted into our comfortable consciousness. Like September 11 and, now, July 7 as well, it stands in the landscape or the map, a feature that will never be obliterated. That was when things changed.

Anniversaries are among the things we most take for granted, in our personal lives (birthdays and wedding anniversaries) and in public life (November 5th, Remembrance Day). This last year, we have been marking 200 years since Trafalgar and 60 years since the end of the Second World War. It's all the more strange, then, that so many are so reluctant to treat Christmas as an anniversary. Just as in the millennium year there was embarrassment about what it actually commemorated, so there is the same embarrassment about the event that Christmas marks. Yet again, we've had the reports of people trying to find ways of turning Christmas into a bland and empty winter jollification. The message seems so often to be, 'Don't remember the story; what matters isn't the real history of the world but just the cycle of the seasons. You only need to remember last year – it got cold and dark and then it started getting warmer and lighter again.' How very bizarre that the most enlightened and progressive thinking of the Western world should take us back to the mind-set of the cavemen!

All right; but why remember the story exactly? Just as a heart-warming tale of a vulnerable baby? There are plenty of other stories about that. What was it that changed when this particular baby was born in Bethlehem? Why is it a vital part of the story of the whole world? Christians have a quite elaborate answer, in terms of how this was the moment when God began to live as a human being, began to live the life that led to his redeeming death and transforming resurrection. But, just for a minute, put this on hold. If you were an unbeliever or half-believer, what might convince you that this did indeed mark a change so significant that we'd still be thinking about it after two thousand years?

'Everything necessary has been given us in the Gospels. What is it? Firstly, the love of one's neighbour – the supreme form of living energy. Once it fills the heart of man it has to overflow and spend itself. And secondly, the two concepts which are the main part of the make-up of modern man – without them he is inconceivable – the ideas of free personality and of life regarded as sacrifice.' Words from one of the great novels of the twentieth century, a novel born out of the nightmare conditions of modern totalitarianism – Pasternak's *Dr Zhivago*. Again and again in this astonishing work, Pasternak returns to the point, the point of vision that gave him his own personal resource to fight back against the pressure to silence and conformity in Stalin's Russia.

'Something in the world had been changed. Rome was at an end. The reign of numbers was at an end. … The story of a human life became the life story of God and filled the universe.'

What has changed? 'Rome was at an end' says Pasternak's character. Christ was born into a society we can hardly imagine (though a somewhat lurid television series this autumn has captured some of it), in which any notion of the sanctity of every life was completely alien; some were born only to die – handicapped children, girl children in some places, exposed on hillsides to starve or freeze; slaves who existed to serve every passing desire of their masters and mistresses; outsiders, foreigners, who were not really human; gladiators whose job it was to kill or be killed for public amusement. It's not – let's be clear – that human behaviour has improved so spectacularly since the first Christmas that we can look back on these atrocities with complacency. A country with our current rates of abortion cannot afford to rest on its ethical laurels; there is effective slavery among the poorest of our world; civilized societies have started flirting once again with the idea that torture might be acceptable. It isn't that we have left Roman-style inhumanity entirely behind; what has changed is that no-one now could possibly take these things for granted without coming up against a challenge from most of the main imaginative and moral currents of our European and Middle Eastern cultural history.

In other words, you may or may not believe what Christian doctrine says about the child in the manger; but you will, consciously or not, be looking at the human world in a framework that Jesus Christ made possible – which is, incidentally, quite a good reason for thinking twice before rejecting the doctrine. A vision has been introduced into the world that cannot be expelled. We talk boldly – and for the most part rightly – about how we can't turn the clock back with ideals of democracy and accountability and freedom of conscience. No-one can pretend they haven't been thought about and in some degree realized among us. True; but what about the fact that, ultimately, made all of them possible, the fact that put an end to Rome, to the age of unquestioned, inhuman empires and mass deaths that gave no-one any sleepless nights?

Sometimes today you can just faintly hear voices whispering that perhaps there was something to be said for the ancient world; that universal human dignity and the absolute wrongness of certain acts of violence and cruelty are nice ideas but a bit difficult in a complicated world. God forgive us. But if we do ever come to forget not just the Christmas story but what it made possible, the end of Rome, the arrival of a different humanity, there is enough, sadly, in our idle and self-obsessed hearts to let the ancient world begin to creep back a little bit more.

I don't believe that in fact it could be possible to forget. When modern tyrannies have tried to make people forget, memory has shown itself pretty tenacious, secretly, obstinately, subversively. After all, if it's simply true that Jesus was born and lived and died and rose as he did, things just have changed; you can deny that the sun has risen if you like, but only by insisting on keeping your eyes tight shut. All around, the landscape has changed, and people are discovering that they are capable of living differently in the company of Jesus.

A few weeks ago, Gee Walker, mother of the murdered Liverpool teenager Anthony Walker, told us that yes, she forgave her son's killers and yes, her heart was still broken. What made this so intensely moving was the fact that her forgiveness was drawn agonizingly out of her, without making her loss easier. She could not have been who she was if she did not recognize that forgiveness was laid upon her; her life and her dead son's would have been nonsense if she did not forgive. It was mercy without a hint of trivialization or excuse for wrongdoing. No preacher could say it like that, could make it sound utterly true and costly and necessary all at once.

And last week, the mother of Abigail Witchall, paralysed by a knife attack in April, described her sadness about Abigail's attacker, who had killed himself: 'his death is the real tragedy in this story', she wrote, not making light of her daughter's terrible ordeal or denying the complex evil of the action, but simply making space in her heart for someone else's fear and pain.

Why remember what happened at Bethlehem, why resist the efforts to reduce it to a brief fling of sentimental goodwill in the middle of bad weather? Because of people like these. They have known in their flesh and nerves just what the difference is that Jesus makes; it is not

comfort or easy answers, it is the sheer fact that
– we have to use the word – miraculous love is
possible. The vilest offender, as the hymn says,
is now deserving of attention and compassion;
no life can be allowed to fall out of the circle of
love. Because God has overthrown the empire
of numbers and calculations, mass movements
and majority interests: 'The story of a human
life became the life story of God and filled the
universe.' Remember this day; this was when the
new creation began.

THE POOREST DESERVE
THE BEST

Christmas 2006

Three days ago in Bethlehem, I was holding a new-born baby in my arms. He had been abandoned by his mother, found by the side of the road and taken into the St Vincent Crèche, attached to Holy Family Hospital – along with dozens of other children who had been similarly abandoned, usually because they'd been born to single mothers in what's often still a fiercely patriarchal and puritanical society. But other stories from the crèche and the wards remind you of some of the even bigger challenges of the region.

The hospital has the best-resourced maternity unit in the whole of the West Bank, equal to the best in Israel. (I was on a pilgrimage to Bethlehem with my fellow presidents of Churches Together in England, Cardinal Murphy-O'Connor, David Coffey of the Baptist Union, and Bishop Nathan of the Armenian Orthodox and some other colleagues.) We were privileged to be taken into the intensive care unit to see babies born at 25 weeks who had survived, thanks to the care offered by the astonishing staff of this institution. But because of the current storms of political conflict within Palestine, and the local and international sanctions against the Palestinian government, no-one is sure where the next month's salary is coming from. For the state-of-the-art equipment, they depend on foreign donations. Keeping a child alive in the neonatal units costs at the very least hundreds of dollars a day, and there is no governmental budget to help. All of us in our group of pilgrims felt that we were witnessing a continuing miracle of dedication, achieving standards any British hospital would be proud of with next to no reliable fall-back in financial and organizational terms.

And what stuck in my mind – and I'm sure the minds of my colleagues – was a remark made by Dr Robert Tabash, the medical director, as we stood over an incubator in the intensive care ward. All of this was important, he said, simply because 'the poorest deserve the best' (I promised I would quote him today by name; it's the least I can do to give him the honour he merits). 'The poorest deserve the best': when you hear that, I wonder if you can take in just how revolutionary it is. They do not deserve what's left over when the more prosperous have had their fill, or what can be patched together on a minimal budget as some sort of damage limitation. And they don't 'deserve' the best because they've worked for it and everyone agrees they've earned it. They deserve it simply because their need is what it is and because where human dignity is least obvious it's most important to make a fuss about it. And – to put it as plainly as possible – this is probably the most radically unique and new thing Christmas itself brings into the world.

The Gospel of Jesus Christ tells us that, in God's economy, the overflow of riches happens where the need is greatest; where human dignity is most obscured, grace blazes out in excessive and extravagant ways to remedy the balance. In one famous passage in the Old Testament, God tells his people that they have been chosen precisely because they were the weakest and most helpless community around, slaves and exiles. St Paul – tactful as ever – in his first letter to his converts at Corinth reminds them that they represent the dregs of the urban population. And the one who was born at Bethlehem on Christmas Day rounded on the prosperous and righteous of his times and said, 'You can look after yourselves; the others can't'.

The poorest deserve the best. But, as Jesus clearly knew, poverty has many faces. And the great simplicity of the Gospel's words has to deal with the terrible complexity of situations where different communities experience different kinds of 'poverty' and conflicts of interests and priority arise. Nowhere is this more agonizing than in the Holy Land. No European can or should forget that the state of Israel exists because the Western powers determined after the last war that the Jewish people deserved the best. Their culture, their history, their lives had been ravaged in ways the rest of us could barely imagine. What could be done for a people whose poverty was such that they had no homeland, who had lived for centuries as largely unwelcome guests among other nations and who, when the nightmare began, had no doors of their own to close against a murdering enemy? Today, behind the façade of a 'normal', prosperous Israeli state, that kind of poverty is remembered and felt more bitterly than ever.

Cross the frontier, the frontier marked by the security barrier, and you see the other sorts of poverty: the soaring unemployment, the unpaid teachers and nurses, the people who cannot travel to their farms and olive groves because of the wall. No normality here. And for every young Palestinian passionately committed to staying in the place of their birth to serve their people, there are many whose anger builds daily, poisoning their lives and steering them towards a politics of despair and violence.

The poorest deserve the best. So who 'deserves' our support? Never mind the politics for now. As soon as we try to sort out which we give the advantage to we shall be deciding to some extent who we're against; and that will undoubtedly create another round of poverty and anger and bitterness.

One of the most chilling things on this journey to the Holy Land was the almost total absence in both major communities of any belief that there was a political solution to hand. So step back from that for a moment and ask, 'What do both the communities in the Holy Land ask from us – not just from that convenient abstraction, the "international community", but from you and me?' Both deserve the best. And the best we can give them in such circumstances is at least the assurance of friendship. Go and see, go and listen. Let them know, Israelis and Palestinians alike, that they will be heard and not forgotten. Both communities in their different ways dread – with good reason – a future in which they will be allowed to disappear while the world looks elsewhere. The beginning of some confidence in the possibility of a future is the assurance that there are enough people in the world committed to not looking away and pretending it isn't happening. It may not sound like a great deal, but it is open to all of us to do. And without friendship, it isn't possible to ask of both communities the hard questions that have to be asked, the questions about the killing of the innocent and the brutal rejection of each other's dignity and liberty.

It is open to us; and for us as Christians it is imperative. 'The poorest deserve the best' is one of the things that we know with utter certainty in the light of Christmas and its good news. The tragedies of the Holy Land are not the problems of exotic barbarians far away; they are signs of the underlying tragedies that cripple all human life, individual and collective. Every wall we build to defend ourselves and keep out what may destroy us is also a wall that keeps us in and that will change us in ways we did not choose or want. Every human solution to fears and threats generates a new set of fears and threats. Whether we are thinking of security barriers, Trident missiles or simply the tactics we use as individuals to keep each other at a safe distance, the same shadow appears. Defences do some terrible things to us as well as to our real and imagined enemies.

Humanity itself suffers from poverty, the moral and imaginative poverty that time and again reproduces the same patterns of fear and violence. That beautiful carol, 'This is the truth sent from above', speaks of our history as one of 'ruin' – Adam and Eve 'ruined all, both you and me / And all of their posterity', so that 'We were heirs to endless woes'. The family fortune has been lost. Whether we know it or not, the inheritance of humanity, the birthright of humanity, has been squandered. We were born to glory, to the dignity of being God's children, free and loving and joyful; but the accounts are in the red, the capital is tied up, we don't know what there is for the future.

> We were heirs to endless woes
> Till God the Lord did interpose.

The poorest deserved the best in God's eyes. Not because we had earned it and everyone agreed that it was right and proper, but because God saw the depth of our human tragedy and his power and glory overflowed into that dark space, into that ruined depth. Not one of us, not even the most confident law keeping and godly person, can in truth look after themselves. When Jesus has reproached the respectable who complain that he spends all his time with the unrespectable, he lets them know that if they could just recognize their own poverty, he would be with them at once with the same compassion. We have betrayed our dignity and wasted our inheritance. And God does not let us have what's left over from the grace given to holy and honourable people. He doesn't look around for some small bonus that might come from the end-of-year surplus in the budget. He gives the best: himself; his life, his presence, in his eternal Son and Word. He gives Jesus to be born, to die and rise again and to call us into full fellowship with him in the Spirit. He gives us his own passion and urgency to go where human dignity is most threatened and pour out extravagantly the riches of love.

The poorest deserve the best. Our world and our nation are not organized on that principle and perhaps they never will be. But the truth doesn't change, 'the truth sent from above', about our own universal ruin and restoration and about what that lays upon us when we look at the various specific poverties we confront in our human family. We revert so readily to the idea that love must go where merit lies, that help must follow merit and achievement. But God thinks otherwise it seems.

The child I held last Friday had no merits and achievements. He deserved the best in spite of – or because of? – having nothing but his helplessness. We are used at Christmas to singing about the poor helpless child of Bethlehem whom we will cradle and rock and keep warm. But the great mystery of the day, the joy and shock of it, is that it is Jesus Christ who picks us up, helpless children, abandoned, ruined, and promises us everything that he can give. And as he gives, he makes us grow, and sends us to make the same promise in his name to all, whatever the conflicts, whatever the guilt. To all he offers the authority to be children of God; from his fullness we may all receive grace upon grace.

THE MARRIAGE OF HEAVEN AND EARTH

Christmas 2007

Eleven days ago, the Church celebrated the memory of the sixteenth century Spanish saint, John of the Cross, Juan de Yepes – probably the greatest Christian mystical writer of the last thousand years, a man who worked not only for the reform and simplification of the monastic life of his time but also for the purification of the inner life of Christians from fantasy, self-indulgence and easy answers. Those who've heard of him will most likely associate him with the phrase that he introduced into Christian thinking about the hard times in discipleship – 'the dark night of the soul'. He is a ruthless analyst of the ways in which we prevent ourselves from opening up to the true joy that God wants to give us by settling for something less than the real thing and confusing the truth and grace of God with whatever makes us feel good or comfortable. He is a disturbing and difficult writer; not, you'd imagine, a man to go to for Christmas good cheer.

But it was St John who left us, in some of his poems, one of the most breathtakingly imaginative visions ever of the nature of Christmas joy, and who, in doing this, put his own analyses of the struggles and doubts of the life of prayer and witness firmly into an eternal context. He is recognized as one of the greatest poets in the Spanish language; and part of his genius is to use the rhythms and conventions of popular romantic poetry and folksong to convey the biblical story of the love affair between God and creation.

One of his sequences of poetry is usually called simply the 'Romances'. It's a series of 75 short, mostly four-line verses, written in the simplest possible style and telling the story of the world from the beginning to the first Christmas – but very daringly telling this story from God's point of view. It begins like a romantic ballad. 'Once upon a time', God was living eternally in heaven, God the Father, the Son and the Holy Spirit, with perfect love flowing uninterrupted between them. And out of the sheer overflowing energy of his love, God the Father decides that he will create a 'Bride' for his Son. The imagery is powerful and direct: there will be someone created who will be able, says God the Father, to 'sit down and eat bread with us at one table, the same bread that I eat.'

And so the world is made as a home for the Bride. Who is this Bride? It is the whole world of beings who are capable of love and understanding, the angels and the human race. In the rich diversity of the world, the heavens and the earth together, God makes an environment in which love and intelligence may grow, until they are capable of receiving the full impact of God's presence. And so the world waits for the moment when God can at last descend and – in a beautiful turning upside down of the earlier image – can sit at the same table and share the same bread as created beings.

As the ages pass on earth, the longing grows and intensifies for this moment to arrive; and at last God the Father tells the Son that it is time for him to meet his Bride face to face on earth, so that, as he looks at her directly, she may reflect his own likeness. When God has become human, then humanity will recognize in his face, in Jesus' face, its own true nature and destiny. And the angels sing at the wedding in Bethlehem, the marriage of heaven and earth, where, in the haunting final stanza of the great poetic sequence, humanity senses the joy of God himself, and the only one in the scene who is weeping is the child, the child who is God in the flesh: 'The tears of man in God, the gladness in man, the sorrow and the joy that used to be such strangers to each other.'

Well, that is how John of the Cross sets out the story of creation and redemption, the story told from God's point of view. And there are two things in this that are worthy of our thoughts and our prayers today. The first is one of the strangest features of John's poems. The coming of Christ is not first and foremost a response to human crisis; there is remarkably little about sin in these verses. We know from elsewhere that John believed what all Christians believe about sin and forgiveness; and even in these poems there is reference to God's will to save us from destruction. But the vision takes us further back into God's purpose. The whole point of creation is that there should be persons, made up of spirit and body, in God's image and likeness, to use the language of Genesis and of the New Testament, who are capable of intimacy with God – not so that God can gain something but so that these created beings may live in joy. And God's way of making sure that this joy is fully available is to

Nativity, from a Book of Hours printed by Philippe Pigouchet for Simon Vostre, 1498 (vellum), MS 1488.5, French School, (15th century)/© Lambeth Palace Library, London, UK.

The Adoration of the Shepherds, 1646 (oil on canvas), Rembrandt Harmensz. van Rijn (1606–69)/Alte Pinakothek, Munich, Germany/Interfoto/The Bridgeman Art Library.

join humanity on earth so that human beings may recognize what they are and what they are for. The sinfulness, the appalling tragedy of human history has set us at what from our point of view seems an unimaginable distance from God; yet God, we might say, takes it in his stride. It means that when he appears on earth he takes to himself all the terrible consequences of where we have gone wrong – 'the tears of man in God'; yet it is only a shadow on the great picture, which is unchanged.

We are right to think about the seriousness of sin, in other words; but we see it properly and in perspective only when we have our eyes firmly on the greatness and unchanging purpose of God's eternal plan for the marriage of heaven and earth. It is a perspective that is necessary when our own sins or those of a failing and suffering world fill the horizon for us, so that we can hardly believe the situation can be transformed. For if God's purpose is what it is, and if God has the power and freedom to enter our world and meet us face to face, there is nothing that can destroy that initial divine vision of what the world is for and what we human beings are for. Nothing changes, however far we fall; if we decide to settle down with our failures and give way to cynicism and despair, that is indeed dreadful – but God remains the same God who has decided that the world should exist so that it may enter into his joy. At Christmas, when this mystery is celebrated, we should above all renew our sheer confidence in God. In today's Bethlehem, still ravaged by fear and violence, we can still meet the God who has made human tears his own and still works ceaselessly for his purpose of peace and rejoicing, through the witness of brave and loving people on both sides of the dividing wall.

But the second point growing out of this is of immense practical importance. The world around us is created as a framework within which we may learn the first beginnings of growing up towards what God wants for us. It is the way it is so that we can be directed towards God. And so this is how we must see the world. Yes, it exists in one sense for humanity's sake; but it exists in its own independence and beauty for humanity's sake – not as a warehouse of resources to serve humanity's selfishness. To grasp that God has made the material world, 'composed', says John of the Cross, 'of infinite differences' so that human beings can see his glory, is to

accept that the diversity and mysteriousness of
the world around is something precious in itself.
To reduce this diversity and to try and empty
out the mysteriousness is to fail to allow God
to speak through the things of creation as he
means to. 'My overwhelming reaction is one of
amazement. Amazement, not only at the extravaganza of details that we have seen; amazement
too, at the very fact that there are any such details
to be had at all, on any planet. The universe
could so easily have remained lifeless and simple.
… Not only is life on this planet amazing, and
deeply satisfying, to all whose senses have not
become dulled by familiarity: the very fact that we
have evolved the brain power to understand our
evolutionary genesis redoubles the amazement
and compounds the satisfaction.' The temptation
to quote Richard Dawkins from the pulpit is
irresistible; in this amazement and awe, if not
in much else, he echoes the sixteenth century
mystic.

So to think of our world as a divine 'prompt' to
our delight and reverence, so that its variety, the
'extravaganza of details', is a precious thing, is to
begin to be committed to that reverent guardi-
anship of this richness that is more and more

clearly required of us as we grow in awareness of how fragile all this is, how fragile is the balance of species and environments in the world and how easily our greed distorts it. When we threaten the balance of things, we don't just put our material survival at risk; more profoundly, we put our spiritual sensitivity at risk, the possibility of being opened up to endless wonder by the world around us.

And it hardly needs adding that this becomes still more significant when we apply John of the Cross's vision to our human relations. Every person and every diverse sort of person exists for a unique joy, the joy of being who they are in relation to God, a joy which each person will experience differently. And when I encounter another, I encounter one who is called to such a unique joy; my relation with them is part of God's purpose in bringing that joy to perfection – in me and in the other. This doesn't rule out the tension and conflict that are unavoidable in human affairs – sometimes we challenge each other precisely so that we can break through what it is in each other that gets in the way of God's joy, so that we can set each other free for this joy.

This, surely, is where peace on earth, the peace the angels promise to the shepherds, begins, here and nowhere else, here where we understand what human beings are for and what they can do for each other. The delighted reverence and amazement we should have towards the things of creation is intensified many times where human beings are concerned. And if peace is to be more than a pause in open conflict, it must be grounded in this passionate amazed reverence for others.

The birth of Jesus, in which that power that holds the universe together in coherence takes shape in history as a single human body and soul, is an event of cosmic importance. It announces that creation as a whole has found its purpose and meaning, and that the flowing together of all things for the joyful transfiguration of our humanity is at last made visible on earth.

'So God henceforth will be human, and human beings caught up in God. He will walk around in their company, eat with them and drink with them. He will stay with them always, the same for ever alongside them, until this world is wrapped up and done with.'

Glory to God in the highest,
and peace on earth to those who are
God's friends.

GLOBAL SAVIOURS,
MORTAL MESSIAHS

Christmas 2008

'There went out a decree from Caesar Augustus'; we've very likely heard those words many, many times in carol services, like an overture to the great drama of the Christmas story. The emperor Augustus would have been delighted, I'm sure, to be told that his name would still be recalled after twenty centuries – but more than a little dismayed that it would be simply because he happened to be around at the time of Christ's birth. There were all sorts of things for which he would have wanted to be remembered, and many of his contemporaries were not slow in telling him about them. And in fairness he had quite a good claim to fame: he had, after all, restored order to the Roman state and consolidated its global influence as never before. For many decades, a kind of peace prevailed from Germany to Syria – enforced by typical Roman brutality when any signs of dissent appeared, but still probably better than the chaos of the Roman civil war that had been going on before. It made sense to hail him as restorer of peace, and to look forward to a long period of stability and prosperity.

It didn't turn out quite like that, of course; but Augustus's reign was for many people a sort of golden age. In later generations, new emperors set themselves the goal of bringing back something of that stability and confidence, and they would describe themselves on their coins and statues as the rescuers of the world's good order – as 'saviours': something that had already been common among the kings of the Middle East in earlier centuries.

So if you'd asked people of Jesus' day what the word 'saviour' meant, the answer would be pretty plain. It was someone who would bring back the golden age, who would put an end to conflict; you could almost say it was someone who would stop things happening. Salvation was the end of history, brought about by one unique charismatic leader.

Curious that, all these years later, the same language still survives. Twentieth century totalitarian systems looked forward to a state of things where all conflict was over and change and struggle stopped. On the other side, after the end of the Cold War, some scholars were writing about the 'end of history', and an American president spoke of a 'new world order'. In recent weeks, we've seen some of Barack Obama's advisers and colleagues warning about the level of messianic expectation loaded on to the President-elect – wisely recognizing the risks involved in tapping in to this vein of excited imagination always just below the surface of even the most cynical society. We have certainly not, as human beings, grown out of the fascination of saviours who will restore the good times. 'The Lord has bared his arm and is once and for all returning to Zion' (*Isaiah* 52.10) – surely that is real salvation?

And as always the gospel comes in with a sober 'Yes, but ...'. The saviour arrives, but goes unrecognized. He is hidden in the form of poverty and insecurity, a displaced person. Instead of peace and the golden age restored, there is conflict, a trial, a cross and a mysterious new dawn breaking unlike anything that has gone before. He was in the world and the world did not know him. Yet to those who recognize him and trust him, he gives authority (not just 'power', as our translations have

it) to become something of what he is – to share in
the manifesting of his saving work (*John* 1.10–12).

So what's happening here to the idea of a saviour?
The gospel tells us something hard to hear – that
there is *not* going to be a single charismatic leader
or a dedicated political campaign or a war to end
all wars that will bring the golden age; it tells us
that history will end when God decides, not when
we think we have sorted all our problems out;
that we cannot turn the kingdoms of this world
into the kingdom of God and his anointed; that
we cannot reverse what has happened and restore
a golden age. But it tells us something that at the
same time explodes all our pessimism and world-
weariness. There *is* a saviour, born so that all may
have life in abundance, a saviour whose authority
does not come from popularity, problem-solving
or anything else in the human world. He is the
presence of the power of creation itself. He is the
indestructible divine life, and the illumination
he gives cannot be shrouded or defeated by the
darkness of human failure.

But he has become flesh. He has come to live as
part of a world in which conflict comes back again
and again, and history does not stop, a world in

which change and insecurity are not halted by a magic word, by a stroke of pen or sword on the part of some great leader, some genius. He will change the world and – as he himself says later in John's gospel – he will overcome the world simply by allowing into the world the unrestricted force and flood of divine life, poured out in self-sacrifice (*John* 10.9–11). It is not the restoring of a golden age, nor even a return to the Garden of Eden; it is more – a new creation, a new horizon for us all.

And it can be brought into being only in 'flesh'; not by material force, not by brilliant negotiation but by making real in human affairs the depth of divine life and love; by showing 'glory' – the intensity and radiance of unqualified joy, eternal self-giving. Only in the heart of the ordinary vulnerability of human life can this be shown in such a way, so that we are saved from the terrible temptation of confusing it with earthly power and success. This is, in Isaiah's words, 'the salvation *of our God*' – not of anything or anyone else.

For those who accept this revelation and receive the promised authority, what can be done to show his glory? So often the answer to this lies in the small and local gestures, the unique difference made in some particular corner of the world, the way in which we witness to the fact that history not only goes on but is also capable of being shifted towards compassion and hope. This year, as every year, we remember in our prayers the crises and sufferings of the peoples of the Holy Land: how tempting it is to think that somehow there will be a 'saviour' here – a new US president with a fresh vision, an election in Israel or Palestine that will deliver some new negotiating strategy. It's perfectly proper to go on praying for a visionary leadership in all those contexts; but meanwhile, the 'saving' work is already under way, not delayed until there is a comprehensive settlement.

This last year, one of the calendars in my study, one of the things that provides me with images for reflection every day, has been the one issued by Families for Peace – a network of people from both communities in the Holy Land who have lost children or relatives in the continuing conflict; people who expose themselves to the risk of meeting the family of someone who killed their son or daughter, the risk of being asked to sympathize with someone whose son or daughter was killed by activists promoting what you regard as a just cause. The Parents Circle and Families Forum organized by this network are labouring to bring hope into a situation of terrible struggle simply by making the issues 'flesh', making them about individuals with faces and stories. When I have met these people, I have been overwhelmed by their courage; but also left with no illusions about how hard it is, and how they are made to feel again and again that they come to their own and their own refuse to know them. Yet if I had to identify where you might begin to speak of witnesses to 'salvation' in the Holy Land, I should unhesitatingly point to them.

In any such situation, the same holds true. In recent days, I have been catching up with news of other enterprises in the Holy Land, especially from the Christian hospitals in Bethlehem and Nazareth, struggling with all kinds of pressure on them from various sources and with the chronic problem of desperately small resources, yet still obstinately serving all who come to them, from whatever background. And last week I spoke with someone helping to run a small community theatre project in Bulawayo, supported by local churches, working to deepen the confidence and the hope of those living in the middle of some of the worst destitution even Zimbabwe can show. Signs of salvation; not a magical restoration of the golden age, but the stubborn insistence that there is another order, another reality, at work in the midst of moral and political chaos; the reality that is the eternal 'Logos', St John's Greek term that means not simply a word but a pattern of harmonious relation.

That is what is made flesh at Christmas. And our own following of the Word made flesh is what gives us the resources to be perennially suspicious of claims about the end of history or the coming of some other saviour exercising some other sort of power. To follow him is to take the risks of working at these small and stubborn outposts of newness, taking our responsibility and authority. In the months ahead it will mean in our own country asking repeatedly what is asked of us locally to care for those who bear the heaviest burdens in the wake of our economic crisis – without waiting for the magical solution, let alone the return of the good times. Internationally, it is remembering that our personal involvement in prayer and giving is utterly essential, whatever pressure we may rightly want to bring to bear on governments and organisations.

Isaiah looked towards the day when the guards on the deserted city's wall would see the return of the Lord 'face-to-face' (*Isaiah* 52.8). So much of our witness to salvation depends on this face-to-face encounter. We can't pass the buck to Caesar Augustus, Barack Obama or even Canterbury City Council – though we may pray for them all and hope that they will play their part in witnessing to new possibilities. To follow the Word made flesh is to embark, with a fair bit of fear and trembling, it may be, on making history – not waiting for it to stop. And that means speaking and working for Christ in the myriad face-to-face encounters in which he asks us to be his witnesses – to see and to show 'his glory, the glory as of the Father's only Son, full of grace and truth' (*John* 1.14).

THE HEIR OF ALL CREATION

Christmas 2009

This morning's reading from the Letter to the Hebrews (1.1–4) begins with the boldest and most unambiguous statement possible of what's new and different about Christmas. God has always been communicating with humanity, in any number of ways; but what we need from God is more than just information. The climax of the story is the sending of a Son: when all has been said and done on the level of information, what still needs to be made clear to us is that the point of it all is relationship. God speaks at last through a Son, so that we can grasp the fact that really knowing God, really responding to his Word of promise and life, is a matter of relationship. It's becoming God's child. And the consequence is that we ourselves learn to speak and act in such a way that others want to share that relationship.

The Son, says the writer to the Hebrews, is the heir of all creation; the Son is the life-giving principle of all reality; the Son radiates and reflects the unimaginable beauty and light of the source from which he comes. When the Son is born among us, what happens is that this unlimited, unending torrent of light and glory, of intelligence and order and loving contemplation, is poured into the container of a human mind and body. Through what he then does in that human mind and body, the possibilities for human life are changed for ever, and we are invited into the same place in heaven that the Son occupies for ever – the place that St John's gospel defines as 'nearest to the Father's heart' (*John* 1.18). And the letter-writer triumphantly claims that our human destiny is thus to be even closer to God than the angels are. Christian poets and thinkers have often imagined the angels looking at us with amazement – such very unpromising material, such limited capacities, such a genius for self-deception and pettiness, yet promised such a future.

Relationship is the new thing at Christmas, the new possibility of being related to God as Jesus was and is. But here's the catch and the challenge. To come into this glorious future is to learn how to be dependent on God. And that word tends to have a chilly feel for us, especially us who are proudly independent moderns. We speak of 'dependent' characters with pity and concern; we think of 'dependency' on drugs and alcohol; we worry about the 'dependent' mindset that can be created by handouts to the destitute. In other words, we think of dependency as something passive and less than free.

But let's turn this round for a moment. If we think of being dependent on the air we breathe, or the food we eat, things look different. Even more if we remind ourselves that we depend on our parents for learning how to speak and act and above all how to love. There is a dependence that is about simply receiving what we need to live; there is a dependence that is about how we learn and grow. And part of our human problem is that we mix up this entirely appropriate and life-giving dependency with the passivity that can enslave us. In seeking (quite rightly) to avoid passivity we can get trapped in the fantasy that we don't need to receive and to learn.

Which is why it matters that our reading portrays the Son in the way it does – radiant, creative, overflowing with life and intelligence. The Son is all these things because he is dependent, because he receives his life from the Father. And when we finally grow up into the fullness of his life, we shall, like him, be gladly and unashamedly dependent – open to receiving all God has to give, open to learn all he has to teach. This is a 'dependency' that is utterly creative and the very opposite of passive. It is a matter of being aligned with the freest activity we can imagine, God's eternal love, flowing through us.

At some level we all recognize this, because we've all seen something like it at work in our family lives and even our closest friendships. Depending on each other, receiving and learning, are natural things, natural expressions of closeness and trust. Yet we have over the long millennia of human existence created a whole culture in which there is a basic impatience about learning – we want to get to the point where we can say, 'OK, that's enough, I know what I need to know'; and about receiving – 'we don't want to be indebted to others, we want to stand on our own two feet'. Like many in this congregation, I suspect, I can hear voices from my parents' and grandparents' generation saying they don't want charity, they don't want to be beholden, they don't want handouts from the state or anywhere else. There's something brave and admirable about much of this when what it represents is a generous unwillingness to burden others. But it can also reflect a stubborn hankering after a life that is under my management and doesn't need support from outside.

One of the worst effects of this culture of impatience and pride is what it does to those who are most obviously dependent – the elderly, those with physical or psychological challenges and disabilities, and, of course, children. We send out the message that, if you're not standing on your own two feet and if you need regular support, you're an anomaly. We'll look after you (with a bit of a sigh), but frankly it's not ideal. And in the case of children, we shall do our level best to turn you into active little consumers and performers as soon as we can. We shall test you relentlessly in schools, we shall bombard you with advertising, often highly sexualized advertising, we shall worry you about your prospects and skills from the word go, we shall do all we can to make childhood a brief and rather regrettable stage on the way to the real thing – which is 'independence', turning you into a useful cog in the social machine that won't need too much maintenance.

In the last year, the issues around how we regard childhood in our society have been opened up for discussion with new intensity by a number of important pieces of research like the Children's Society's Good Childhood report or the Cambridge Review of primary education. There has at last been a wake-up call about the ways in which we are crushing and narrowing children's experience; and there is a long and significant agenda there for debate in the months ahead.

But, behind the details, there is one central issue. Can we as a society accept and even celebrate the fact that there is a place for proper and mature dependence – that human beings need to receive and learn: not so that they can get to the point where they stop receiving and learning, but so that they can acquire the habits of receiving and learning in ever-new settings? Can we help children enjoy their dependency so that they don't just leave it behind but get to manage it with freedom and imagination as they grow older?

And that involves two difficult lessons for us adults. One is simply to reconnect ourselves to our own capacity to receive and learn with joy and excitement – to become like little children, as somebody once said. The other is to be ready to give the nurture and security that children need – to create the safe places where they can learn, where they can make their mistakes. To do this is to show that we treasure dependency and that we shan't either exploit it or ignore it. Embracing and celebrating our own dependence gives us the vision and energy to make sure that others have the freedom to make the most of their dependence too. And this means working to give all the children of the world the security they need.

In our own society, there are problems enough – children who have never known stability in their family life, who have never known a father or who have been pushed into taking responsibility for a parent or for brothers and sisters, with a mother who is ailing, addicted or otherwise incapacitated; children with workaholic parents, materially well off but deprived of warmth and relaxation with their family; worse still, children and young people who are systematically exploited through sex trafficking, children who are trapped in gang culture. Worldwide, all these problems and more are all too visible; perhaps one of the most appalling phenomena, still affecting hundreds of thousands of children, is the exploiting of children in the meaningless and savage civil wars in places like Congo and Sri Lanka – children who are abducted, brutalized, turned into killers, used as sex slaves. To hear of these experiences is almost unbearable, yet the scandal continues.

These children are created, like all of us, to become fully and consciously children of God, to enjoy that glory we reflected on a few minutes ago. Their suffering is an insult to the purpose of God, a contemptuous refusal of the gift of God on the part of those who keep them in their different kinds of slavery. God's gift at Christmas is relationship, not just another human relationship but relation to God the Father by standing where Jesus stands, standing in the full torrent of his love and creativity, giving and receiving. To come into that place and to be rooted and grounded there means letting go of our fear of dependence and opening our hearts to be fed and enlarged and transformed. And that in turn means looking at how we handle dependence in ourselves and others, how we accept the positive dependence involved in lifelong learning and growing, and help one another deal with it positively.

So the important thing is not that everyone gets to stand on their own two feet and turns into a reliable 'independent' consumer and contributor to the gross national product. What we expect from each other in a generous and grown-up society is much more to do with all of us learning how to ask from each other, how to receive from each other, how to depend on the generosity of those who love us and stand alongside us. And that again means a particular care for those who need us most, who need us to secure their place and guarantee that there is nourishment and stability for them. As we learn how to be gratefully dependent, we learn how to attend to and respond to the dependence of others. Perhaps by God's grace we shall learn in this way how to create a society in which real dependence is celebrated and safeguarded, not regarded with embarrassment or abused by the powerful and greedy.

God has spoken through a Son. He has called us all to become children at the cradle of the Son, the Word made flesh, so that we may grow into a glory that even the angels wonder at. To all who accept him he gives power and authority to become children of God, learning and growing into endless life and joy.

GREAT IS THY FAITHFULNESS

Christmas 2010

'This was to fulfill what the Lord had spoken through the prophet' (*Matthew* 1.22). Phrases like this echo like a refrain through the nativity stories in the Gospels – and indeed the stories of Jesus' trial and death as well. The stories of Jesus' birth and death were, from the very first, stories about how God had kept his promise. The earliest Christians looked at the records and memories of what had happened in and around the life of Jesus and felt a sense of *déjà vu*: doesn't this remind you of …? Surely this is the same as …?

Bit by bit, they connected up the details of the stories with a rich pattern of events and images and ideas in Hebrew Scripture. Utterly unexpected pregnancies – like Abraham's wife Sarah, or Hannah, mother of the prophet Samuel. A birth in Bethlehem, the place where Jacob's wife died in bringing to birth the last of the ancestors of Israel, where an impoverished young widow from an enemy country was welcomed and made at home, to become the grandmother of the great hero King David. Shepherds in the fields of Bethlehem where young David had looked after his father's flock before being called to be shepherd of the whole kingdom. A star like the one foreseen by the ancient prophet Balaam as a sign of Israel's victory; foreigners bringing gifts of gold and incense, as the psalm describes foreign potentates bringing tribute to King Solomon. A murderous attack on the children of God's people by a Godless tyrant; a desperate flight and an exile in Egypt. The plain event at the centre of it all, the birth of a child in a jobbing handyman's family, is surrounded with so many echoes and allusions that it seems like the climax of an immense series of great happenings; like the final statement in a musical work of some theme that has been coming through again and again, more and more strongly, in the earlier bars. The last triumphant movement in God's symphony.

The story of Jesus is the story of a God who keeps promises. As St Paul wrote to the Corinthians, 'however many the promises God made, the Yes to them all is in him' (*2 Corinthians* 1.20). God shows himself to be the same God he always was. He brings hope out of hopelessness – out of the barrenness of unhappy childless women like Sarah and Hannah. He takes strangers and makes them at home; he brings his greatest gifts out of those moments when the barriers are down between insiders and outsiders. He draws people from the ends of the earth to wonder – not this time at the glory of Solomon but at the miracle of his presence among the humble and outcast. He identifies with those, especially children, who are the innocent and helpless victims of insane pride and fear. He walks into exile with those he loves and leads them home again.

This is the God he has shown himself to be; and he has promised that he will go on being the same God. 'I am who I am', he tells us; and 'I, the Lord, do not change', and 'I will not fail you or forsake you'. When we are faithless, he is faithful; when we seek to escape or even to betray, he does not change. In what is perhaps the most unforgettable image in the whole of Hebrew Scripture, God says that he has 'branded' or 'engraved' us on the palms of his hands (*Isaiah* 49.16). He has determined that he will not be who he is without us. And in this moment of climax and fulfilment, in this last movement of the symphony, he shows in the most decisive way possible that he will not be without us; he binds his divine life to human

81

nature. Never again can he be spoken of except in connection with this human life that begins in the stable at Bethlehem.

From one point of view, then, a story of triumphant persistence. Nothing has shaken God's decision to be with those he has loved and called, and now nothing ever will. Nothing, as St Paul again says, can separate us from what is laid bare in the life and death and resurrection of Jesus (*Romans* 8.38–39). And yet, from another point of view, it is a story of unimaginable cost and apparent tragedy. For if God has chosen to be with us in this way, he is associated with our weaknesses, humiliated by our betrayals, exposed and vulnerable to our casual decisions to take our custom elsewhere. In the book of the prophet Hosea, we see this depicted in harrowing terms as the marriage of a faithful man to an unfaithful woman, a marriage that the man refuses to accept is over. I suspect that a good many of us have seen cases of a faithful woman sticking obstinately to an unfaithful man. In human terms, such faithfulness is likely to look naïve, foolish or just pointless self-punishing. But God, it seems, knows that whatever limitation and humiliation our human freedom lays on him, we cannot live without him; and he accepts everything for the sake of our well being.

Christmas is about the unshakeable solidarity of God's love with us, not only in our suffering but in our rebellion and betrayal as well. One mediaeval Greek theologian, deliberately out to shock, described it as God's *manike eros* – 'manic passion', God's 'obsession'. And so it is a time to do some stocktaking about our own solidarity and fidelity, our own promise-keeping.

There are at least three things we might ponder in that respect, seeking to understand ourselves better in the light of the Christmas story. The first is our solidarity with one another, in our society and our world, our solidarity with and loyalty to our fellow citizens and fellow human beings. Faced with the hardship that quite clearly lies ahead for so many in the wake of financial crisis and public spending cuts, how far are we able to sustain a living sense of loyalty to each other, a real willingness to bear the load together? How eager are we to find some spot where we feel safe from the pressures that are crippling and terrifying others? As has more than once been said, we can and will as a society bear hardship if we are confident that it is being fairly shared; and we shall have that confidence only if there are signs that everyone is committed to their neighbour, that no-one is just forgotten, that no interest group or pressure group is able to opt out. That confidence isn't in huge supply at the moment, given the massive crises of trust that have shaken us all in the last couple of years and the lasting sense that the most prosperous have yet to shoulder their load. If we are ready, if we are *all* ready, to meet the challenge represented by the language of the 'big society', we may yet restore some mutual trust. It's no use being cynical about this; whatever we call the enterprise, the challenge is the same – creating confidence by sharing the burden of constructive work together.

The second is something quite different, but no less challenging. Next year, we shall be joining in the celebration of what we hope will be a profoundly joyful event in the royal wedding. It is certainly cause for celebration that any couple, let alone this particular couple, should want to embark on the adventure of Christian marriage, because any and every Christian marriage is a sign of hope, since it is a sign and sacrament of God's own committed love. And it would be good to think that in this coming year, we, as a society, might want to think through, carefully and imaginatively, why lifelong faithfulness and the mutual surrender of selfishness are such great gifts. If we approach this in the light of what we have just been reflecting on in terms of the Christmas story of a promise-keeping God, we shall have no illusions about how easy it is to sustain such long-term fidelity and solidarity. There will be times when we may feel stupid or helpless; when we don't feel we have the energy or resource to forgive and rebuild after a crisis or a quarrel; when we don't want our freedom limited by the commitments we've made to someone else. Yet many of us will know marriages where something extraordinary has happened because of the persistence of one of the parties, or where faithfulness has survived the tests of severe illness or disability or trauma. I admit, I find myself deeply moved at times when I speak with the families of servicemen and women, where this sense of solidarity is often so deeply marked, so generous and costly. As the prince and his fiancée get ready for their new step into solidarity together, they will have plenty of inspiration around, more than you might sometimes guess from the chatter of our culture. And we can all share the recognition that, without the inspiration of this kind of commitment in marriage, our humanity would be a lot duller and more shallow – and, for the believer, a lot less transparent to the nature of the God who keeps his covenant.

And lastly – a point that we rightly return to on every great Christian festival – there is our solidarity with those of our brothers and sisters elsewhere in the world who are suffering for their Christian faith or their witness to justice or both. Yet again, I remind you of our Zimbabwean friends, still suffering harassment, beatings and arrests, legal pressures and lockouts from their churches; of the dwindling Christian population in Iraq, facing more and more extreme violence from fanatics – and it is a great grace that both Christians and Muslims in this country have joined in expressing their solidarity with this beleaguered minority. Our prayers continue for Asia Bibi in Pakistan and others from minority groups who suffer from the abuse of the law by certain groups there. We may feel powerless to help; yet we should also know that people in such circumstances are strengthened simply by knowing they have not been forgotten. And if we find we have time to spare for joining in letter-writing campaigns for all prisoners of conscience, Amnesty International and Christian Solidarity worldwide will have plenty of opportunities for us to make use of.

Economic justice and Christian marriage and solidarity with the persecuted: very diverse causes, you might think. But, in each case, the key point is about keeping faith, sharing risks, recognizing that our lives belong together. And all this is rooted for us in that event in which all God's purposes, all God's actions, what we might call all God's 'habits of behaviour' with us come into the clearest focus. 'This was to fulfil what the Lord had spoken'; this was the 'Yes' to all the promises. And what God showed himself to be in Hebrew Scripture, what he showed himself to be in the life and death of the Lord Jesus, this is what he has promised to be today and tomorrow and for ever. He cannot betray his own nature, and so he cannot betray us. And by the gift of the Spirit, we are given strength, in all these contexts we have considered and many more, to let his faithful love flow through us, for the fulfilment of more and more human lives according to his eternal purpose and unshakeable love.

THE WORD OF LIFE,
THE WORDS OF PRAYER

Christmas 2011

When the first Christians read – or more probably heard – the opening words of John's gospel ('In the beginning was the Word. The Word was with God, and the Word was God.'), they would have understood straight away quite a lot more than we do. They would have remembered, many of them, that in Hebrew 'word' and 'thing' are the same, and they would all have known that in Greek the word used (*logos*) has a huge range of meaning – at the simplest level, just something said; but also a pattern, a rationale, as we might say, even the entire structure of the universe seen as something that makes sense to us, the structure that holds things together and makes it possible for us to think.

Against this background, we can get a glimpse of just what is being said about Jesus. His life is what God says and what God does; it is the life in which things hold together; it is because of the life that lives in him that we can think. Jesus is the place where all reality is focused, brought to a point. Here is where we can see as nowhere else what connects all reality – all human experience and all natural laws. Edward Elgar famously said about his Enigma Variations that they were all based on a tune that everyone knew – and no-one has ever worked out what tune he meant. But John's gospel declares that the almost infinite variety of the life we encounter is all variations on the theme that is stated in one single clear musical line, one melody, in the life of Jesus of Nazareth. 'In him was life, and the life was the light of men.'

But this shouldn't make us forget entirely the underlying image. The life that lives in Jesus, the everlasting divine agency that is uniquely embodied in him, is like something that is said – a word addressed to us. Because, like any word addressed to us, it demands a response. And the gospel goes on at once to tell us that the expected response was not forthcoming. Before we have even got to Christmas in the words of the gospel, we are taken to Good Friday, and to the painful truth that the coming of Jesus splits the world into those who respond and those who don't. Once the word is spoken in the world, there is no way back. Your response to it, says the gospel again and again, is what shows who and what you really are, what is deepest in you, what means most. What we say or do in our response to Jesus is our way of discovering for ourselves and showing to one another what is real in and for us. Like the other gospel writers, John hints very strongly that some people respond deeply and truthfully to Jesus without fully knowing who he is or what exactly they are doing in responding to him; this is not a recipe for tight religious exclusivism. But the truth is still an uncompromising one: if you cannot or will not respond, you are walking away from reality into a realm of trackless fogbound falsehood.

There is the question we cannot ignore. It's been well said that the first question we hear in the Bible is not humanity's question to God but God's question to us, God walking in the cool of the evening in the Garden of Eden, looking for Adam and Eve who are trying to hide from him. 'Adam, where are you?' (*Genesis* 3.9) The life of Jesus is that question translated into an actual human life, into the conversations and encounters of a flesh-and-blood human being like all others – except that when people meet him they will say, like the woman who talks with him at the well of Samaria, 'Here is a man who told me everything I ever did' (*John* 4.29). Very near the heart of Christian faith and practice is this encounter with God's questions, 'Who are you, where are you?' Are you on the side of the life that lives in Jesus, the life of grace and truth, of unstinting generosity and unsparing honesty, the only life that gives life to others? Or are you on your own side, on the side of disconnection, rivalry, the hoarding of gifts, the obsession with control? To answer that you're on the side of life doesn't mean for a moment that you can now relax into a fuzzy philosophy of 'life-affirming' comfort. On the contrary: it means you are willing to face everything within you that is cheap, fearful, untruthful and evasive, and let the light shine on it. Like Peter in the very last chapter of John's gospel, we can only say that we are trying to love the truth that is in Jesus, even as we acknowledge all we have done that is contrary to his spirit. And we say this because we trust that we are loved by this unfathomable mystery who comes to us in the shape of a newborn child, 'full of grace and truth'.

Finding words to respond to the Word made flesh is and always has been one of the most demanding things human beings can do. Don't believe for a moment that religious language is easier or vaguer than the rest of our language. It's more like the exact opposite. Think of St John writing his gospel, crafting the slow, sometimes repetitive pace of a narrative that allows Jesus to change the perspective inch by inch as a conversation unfolds; or of St Paul, losing his way in his sentences, floundering in metaphors as he struggles to find the words for something so new that there are no precedents for talking about it; or any number of the great poets and contemplatives of the Christian centuries. It isn't surprising if we need other people's words a lot of the time; and it's of great importance that we have words to hand that have been used by others in lives that obviously have depth and integrity.

That's where the language of our shared worship becomes so important. This coming year we celebrate the 350th anniversary of the *Book of Common Prayer*. It has shaped the minds and hearts of millions; and it has done so partly because it has never been a book for individuals alone. It is common prayer, prayer that is shared. In its origins, it was meant to be – and we may well be startled by the ambition of this – a book that defined what a whole society said to God together. If the question 'Where are you?'

or 'Who are you?' were being asked, not only individual citizens of Britain but the whole social order could have replied, 'Here we are, speaking together – to recognize our failures and our ideals, to recognize that the story of the Bible is our story, to ask together for strength to live and act together in faithfulness, fairness, pity and generosity.' If you thumb through the Prayer Book, you may be surprised at how much there is that takes for granted a very clear picture of how we behave with each other. Yes, of course, much of this language feels dated – we don't live in the unselfconscious world of social hierarchy that we meet here. But before we draw the easy and cynical conclusion that the Prayer Book is about social control by the ruling classes, we need to ponder the uncompromising way in which those same ruling classes are reminded of what their power is for, from the monarch downwards. And the almost forgotten words of the Long Exhortation in the Communion Service, telling people what questions they should ask themselves before coming to the sacrament, show a keen critical awareness of the new economic order that, in the mid-sixteenth century, was piling up assets of land and property in the hands of a smaller and smaller elite.

The Prayer Book is a treasury of words and phrases that are still for countless English-speaking people the nearest you can come to an adequate language for the mysteries of faith. It gives us words that say where and who we are before God: 'we have erred and strayed from thy ways like lost sheep', 'we are not worthy so much as to gather up the crumbs under thy table', but also, 'we are very members incorporate in the mystical body of thy Son, which is the blessed company of all faithful people; and are also heirs through hope of the everlasting kingdom'. It gives us words for God that hold on to the paradoxes we can't avoid: 'God ... who art always more ready to hear than we to pray,' 'who declarest thy almighty power most chiefly in showing mercy and pity', 'whose property is always to have mercy'. A treasury of words for God – but also a source of vision for an entire society: 'Give us grace seriously to lay heart the great dangers we are in by our unhappy divisions.' 'If ye shall perceive your offences to be such as are not only against God but also against your neighbours; then ye shall reconcile yourselves unto them; being ready to make restitution.'

The world has changed, the very rhythms of our speech have changed, our society is irreversibly more plural, and we have – with varying degrees of reluctance – found other and usually less resonant ways of talking to God and identifying who we are in his presence. If we used only the Prayer Book these days we'd risk confusing the strangeness of the mysteries of faith with the strangeness of antique and lovely language. But we're much the poorer for forgetting it and pushing it to the margins as much as we often do in the Church. And it is crucial to remember the point about the Prayer Book as something for a whole society, binding together our obligations to God and to one another, in a dense inter-weaving of love and duty joyfully performed.

The Prayer Book was once the way our society found words to respond to the Word, to say who and where they were in answer to God's question, 'where are you?' Those who prayed the Prayer Book, remember, included those who abolished the slave trade and put an end to child labour, because of what they had learned in this book and in their Bibles about the honour of God and of God's children. They knew their story; they knew how to give an answer for themselves, how to join up the muddle of their experience in a coherent pattern by relating it to the unchanging truth and grace of God. That's why the coming year's celebration is not about a museum piece.

The most pressing question we now face, we might well say, is who and where we are as a society. Bonds have been broken; trust is abused and lost. Whether it is an urban rioter mindlessly burning down a small shop that serves his community, or a speculator turning his back on the question of who bears the ultimate cost for his acquisitive adventures in the virtual reality of today's financial world, the picture is of atoms spinning apart in the dark.

And into that darkness the Word of God has entered, in love and judgment, and has not been overcome; in the darkness the question sounds as clear as ever, to each of us and to our Church and our society: 'Britain, where are you?' Where are the words we can use to answer?

STOPPING AND SEEING

Christmas 2012

Fifty-nine per cent of British people describe themselves as Christians, so the census informed us a couple of weeks ago; twelve per cent down from ten years ago. There was, of course, great delight from a couple of secularist organisations. But if I were a member of the British Humanist Association, I might want to pause before I became too excited. It remains true that three quarters of the public still want to identify themselves as having a religious faith of some kind. And what the census doesn't and probably can't measure is exactly how those who don't identify as religious think about religion. Do they never give it a thought? Do they wish they could believe something? Do they see it as a problem or as a resource in society? In the deeply painful aftermath of the Synod's vote last month, what was startling was how many people who certainly wouldn't have said yes to the census question turned out to have a sort of investment in the Church, a desire to see the Church looking credible and a real sense of loss when – as they saw it – the Church failed to sort its business out.

There are a lot more questions to ask before we could possibly assume that the census figures told us that faith was losing its hold on society. But – and here is the challenging thing – what if those figures had been worse? What if they get worse in the next few years? Should we conclude that faith in general and Christian faith in particular had had its day and that we should give up on it? The answer has to be a resounding, 'No: we might feel that we had made a poor job of communicating it, we might regret the enormous loss to public life and public service involved in the weakening of faith. But we simply could *not* conclude that faith had suddenly become impossible or incredible.'

Faith is not about what public opinion decides, and it is not about how we happen to be feeling about ourselves. It is the response people make to what presents itself as a reality – a reality which makes claims on you. Here is something so extraordinary that it interrupts our world; here is something that (like Moses in the story of the Burning Bush) makes you 'turn aside to see', that stops you short. Faith begins in the moment of stopping, you could say: the moment when you can't just walk on as you did before. But even more challengingly, it is something whose claims involve change and even loss. If this is really what it seems to be, ideas, habits, hopes all change, and it is a change that is going to be painful. In the most haunting Christmas poem in the English language [*The Journey of the Magi*], T. S. Eliot imagined the wise men back at home after their journey to Bethlehem, 'no longer at ease here in the old dispensation', and wondering whether what they had witnessed was birth or death.

> ... I had seen birth and death,
> But had thought they were different; this Birth was
> Hard and bitter agony for us, like Death, our death

Yet the wise men can't deny that they've seen what they've seen: they really made the journey and they really saw something that persuaded them it had been worthwhile. Faith: a claim, a shock, a death, a life.

'It was, you may say, satisfactory', says Eliot's wise man, in a masterpiece of Eliot understatement. The wise men found what they were looking for – and it was not at all what they *thought*

101

they had been looking for. The Christian gospel firmly declares two equally necessary truths. Jesus is the hope of the nations, Jesus is what the entire human race really longs to see, the person whose presence heals all wounds and griefs. And Jesus is an utter surprise, so foreign that he is unrecognisable to those who might have been expected to welcome him. He made the world, says St John, and he spoke in its history; but the world had no room for him and the experts in revelation and religious purity turned from him in disgust (*John* 1.10 – 11).You should never open the New Testament without remembering that the religious experts and the Temple hierarchy are the ones who see Jesus as their enemy. They don't want to be interrupted, to stop and see.

The truth of God is the most comforting and joyful presence we can imagine; and also the most disorienting and demanding. There's a famous Old Testament story (*2 Kings* 5) about the great military leader of ancient Israel's fiercest enemy, who comes to the prophet Elisha to be healed of his leprosy; and the prophet tells him simply to wash in the river. He is indignant: surely there must be something more difficult and glamorous and heroic to do? No; it's perfectly simple. Go and wash, go and join all those ordinary humble folk who are sluicing themselves in the river after a long day's work, or beating their laundry against the stones. Go and join the rest of the human race and acknowledge who you are. That's the truest heroism and the hardest.

It's a foreshadowing of the New Testament invitation: repent and believe and be baptised. Turn round and look where you've never looked before, trust the one who is calling you and drop under the water of his overflowing compassion. Be with him. Join the new human race, re-created in the Spirit of mutual love and delight and service.

If Jesus is strange and threatening, isn't that (the New Testament certainly suggests) a sign of how far we've wandered from real humanity, real honesty about our weaknesses and limits? 'I am the great sun, but you do not see me' – the beginning of another wonderful poem, by Charles Causley. We are so fascinated by our own business, whether we call it religious or not, that we find it 'hard and bitter agony' to turn away and be still and look at the mystery of love. If we think about religion, perhaps we think of it as a set of neat answers to our questions, or as a system of behaviour, ritual and moral, or as an optional extra to 'ordinary' life for those who find certain sorts of problem interesting. But Jesus does not come just to answer the questions we think important. (One of the great features of all the gospels, specially St John's, is how often Jesus refuses to answer the question put to him and asks a question in reply.) He does not come to give us a set of techniques for keeping God happy; and he certainly doesn't come to create a harmlessly eccentric hobby for speculative minds. He comes to make humanity itself new, to create fresh possibilities for being at peace with God and each other; and he does this by summoning us to be with him.

It shouldn't surprise us if all this doesn't instantly win the popular vote in a census. If people hesitate to call themselves Christian, perhaps this is a sort of backhanded recognition that there is a strangeness and a toughness to what Christian faith claims that should not be taken lightly. And yet, if many people still do, in spite of everything, want to call themselves by the name Christian, that also means there is a recognition that somehow this is where we should be, where it's *natural* to be – in the company of this man, Jesus Christ, listening to his words, turning aside to *see* deeply into the mysterious events of his life and death and resurrection. But the one thing we can be sure of is that the truth or falsehood of faith doesn't rest on the success of the faith in winning numbers; sometimes this seems to work and sometimes it doesn't. We can and should try as hard and imaginatively as we can to share the faith, but we must not lose heart if it doesn't immediately take root as we might want. We are after all, doing something rather outrageous, asking men and women to stop and look and turn around, and learn how to keep company with a figure whose outlines we often see only dimly.

Yet when a life is lived that shows what that company really means, the outline becomes less dim, and people will begin to recognise why lives like that seem, despite everything, to be 'normal' – the natural response to the way things are. When people respond to outrageous cruelty and violence, with a hard-won readiness to understand and be reconciled, few if any can bring themselves to say that all this is an illusion. The parents who have lost a child to gang violence; the wife who has seen her husband

105

killed in front of her by an anti-Christian mob in India; the woman who has struggled for years to comprehend and accept the rape and murder of her sister; the Israeli and Palestinian friends who have been brought together by the fact that they have lost family members in the conflict and injustice that still racks the Holy Land – all these are specific people I have had the privilege of meeting as archbishop over these ten years; and in their willingness to explore the new humanity of forgiveness and rebuilding relations, without for a moment making light of their own or other people's nightmare suffering, or trying to explain it away, these are the ones who make us see, who oblige us to turn aside and look, as if at a bush burning but not consumed. And to look at Jesus, who asks of us initially just to stop and reflect, to stay for a moment in the light that allows us to see ourselves honestly and to see the world differently.

That's the heart of it, seeing ourselves honestly, seeing the world differently. That's where faith begins, beyond the answers of a system, or the disciplines of a ritual, or the requirements of a moral code. These have their place; and those who spend time in the company of Jesus will find themselves working out all these things in the light of the scriptural witness to the new life. But it all starts with that turning aside to see. And for some, for many perhaps, it is too much to take in, and many will want to turn away. St John describes just this in a later chapter of his gospel (at the end of chapter 6) where Jesus' hearers say that his words are just too much for them, too offensive, too exacting, too weird. Yet if – if we can let go of our conviction that our questions, our priorities and worries, achievements and failures are the most important things in the universe; if we find the freedom to stop and turn aside, then the world itself begins to turn into renewal. 'O come, let us adore him', says the carol. That adoration, that wondering gaze at the child in the manger, is where faith is born; and where faith is born, so is the new world of Jesus and his Spirit.

Easter Sermons

LETTING GO

Easter 2003

> Jesus said, 'Do not cling to me,
> for I have not yet ascended to the
> Father.' (*John* 20.17)

Mary Magdalene wants Jesus back just as she remembers him; failing that, she wants his corpse in a definite place, she wants a grave she can tend. Jesus appears to her – in one of the most devastatingly moving moments of the whole Bible – and her first instinct is to think that, yes, he is back as she remembers, yes, she has hold of him after all. He has not disappeared, he has not been taken away to an unknown destination.

But Jesus warns her: he is being taken to a destination more unknown than she could imagine. He is going to the Father. From now on, there will be no truthful way of speaking or thinking about him except as the one who lives alongside the source of all things. These simple, abrupt words already contain all the mysteries we celebrate when we say the creeds, when we

break the bread of the Holy Communion; they
tell us that Jesus gives exactly what the Father
gives – life, glory, forgiveness, transfiguration.
Through death he has passed into the heart of
reality; he has returned where he came from. At
the very beginning of John's gospel (*John* 1.18),
we read of the Word of God living 'nearest to
the Father's heart' from all eternity. He comes to
us in the flesh and blood of Jesus and shows the
glory, the radiant, solid life, of God pouring out
in love: the fullest showing of that love is in his
free acceptance of suffering and death, and if we
are able to accept that this death sets us free once
and for all, the glory of the divine life is shared
with us. Jesus goes to the Father and from his
place next to the Father's heart sends out the gift
of the Spirit of Truth that allows us a share in his
own closeness to the Father.

Yet to realise this is to realise that we cannot
have Jesus just on our terms. After the resurrection, with its demonstration that Jesus's life
is as indestructible as God the Father's life, we
can't simply go back to the Jesus who is humanly
familiar; and – obviously – we can't have Jesus
as a warm memory, a dear departed whose grave
we can visit. He is alive and ahead of us, clearing

a path to the Father's heart. Christian faith does not look back to a great teacher and example but forward to where Jesus leads, to that ultimate being-at-home with God that he has brought to life in the history of our world.

So: 'Do not cling to me', he says; instead, go, and bring others along on the journey. And Easter always forces us to ask where and how we might want to cling, where and how we might turn away from the task and the journey. There are many ways in which this can happen; I want to think about one in particular, because it has some resonances with where we are at the moment in our national and international life.

There is a clinging to Jesus that shows itself in the longing to be utterly sure of our rightness; we want him there, we want him where we can see him and manage him, so that we know exactly where to turn to be told that everything is all right and that he is on our side. We do it in religious conflicts, we do it in moral debates, we do it in politics. We want to stand still and be reassured, rather than moving faithfully with Jesus along a path into new life whose turnings we don't know in advance. To have an absolute reassurance of our rightness somehow stands in the way of following Jesus to the Father; it offers us an image of ourselves that pleases and consoles, instead of the deeper and harder assurance of the gospel – the assurance that, whether or not we have a satisfying image of ourselves, we have the promise of forgiveness and of a future.

But the temptations go deep. For months now, we have witnessed a profound and disturbing moral argument raging backwards and forwards in this country over the rightness of the war against Iraq. You'll have noticed the way in which some opponents of the war insisted that the motives of those in power must be personally corrupt, greedy, dishonest and bloodthirsty – as if the question could be settled simply by deciding on the wickedness of individuals. Equally though, there have been defenders of the war who have accused its critics of being unable to tell good from evil, of colluding with monstrous cruelty and being indifferent to the suffering of nations. On one side, people seem to see an equivalence between Saddam Hussein and the coalition leaders; on the other, an equivalence between Saddam Hussein and a grandmother from Surrey, a JP and Conservative voter, who finds herself, much to her amazement, on the anti-war march in February. 'Imperialists', 'butchers', cries the one side, 'blood for oil!' 'Appeasers', shouts the other, 'useful idiots.'

This is not simply about how we conduct controversies (though it has some relevance to that, to the barbarous superficiality of some of our public arguments). It is about that odd and not very pleasant tendency in our hearts to ignore the mixture of motives and the uncertainties of understanding that lie behind our own decisions, to deny the elements of chance and hidden prejudice, temperament and feeling that make up our minds, even on the most profound matters. It is about the fear that if we admit this sort of mixture in ourselves we fail to distance ourselves clearly enough from what we believe to be evil. It leads to a further darkening of our minds, as we try to make out that the effects of the war are exactly what would confirm our initial judgements. It is a great victory: 'All the problems will disappear very soon, and reports of regional discontent are much exaggerated.' Or it is a catastrophe: 'We are on the edge of social and political collapse in the Middle East, and the demise of international law.' It is indeed a clinging, a

115

gripping tightly onto whatever perspective we are comfortable with and allowing no time to wait for a fuller discernment to be born. The truth is that we don't yet see clearly. And even if we did, that would not settle the moral rights and wrongs of the conflict's origins.

We cling to what makes us feel most safely distant from evil. The would-be peacemaker is often passionate in treating every kind of force as equally terrible, so that there is a single clear enemy over there to confront – all those with blood on their hands, American general as much as Iraqi executioner. The apologist for war is offended and threatened by the – not unreasonable – suggestion that the motives and methods of modern war are unlikely to be completely shaped by moral considerations, and that fighting evil can involve us in imitating some of its methods, even in the best of causes. Both are afraid of acknowledging that they have something in common with what they are resisting. And that acknowledgement need not lead to despair or passivity (every choice is flawed, I can do nothing just or good); it ought to lead to some kind of adult admission that, even in pursuing good ends, our flawed humanity creates new difficulties. We can only face the possible cost, pray, and trust that God can make use of what we decide and do. Perhaps when Jesus tells us not to cling to him, one of the many things he says is, 'Do not use me, do not use any vision of what is true or good, to keep yourself from recognizing the real and potential evil within you. Don't cling; follow. Take the next step, putting your feet in the gap I have cleared, conscious of how you may make mistakes, but trusting that I can restore you and lead you further, that I can deal with the residues of evil in your heart and in every heart.'

Mary Magdalene tries to cling to a Jesus from the past, her past; her first outburst of joy comes from a conviction that the impossible has happened – that history has been reversed. It hasn't. The crucifixion has happened, and both Jesus' friends and his enemies have made irrevocable decisions in the course of the events around it. Judas and Peter and Pilate will not wake up and find it was all a bad dream. Now, in the light of Easter, they have to decide what to do with their sin and compromise, the past that will not go away, the evil and the mistaken good, the fear and the running away. They, with Magdalene, have to learn that the risen Jesus promises a transformation never yet imagined or expected, the possibility of reconciliation and of sharing Jesus' intimacy with the Father. He is ascending to 'my Father and your Father'. At that moment, neither Mary nor anyone else could know what that would mean; she is called on to go with Jesus so as to discover what it is, and to echo that call in her witness to the apostles, summoning them – and so summoning us – to the Father's heart. On that journey we must travel light, laying aside what one of the desert fathers called the heavy burden of self-justification, and giving up the image of a Jesus who simply assures me of my own image of myself as good and right. From now on, my justification is not that I am proved to have been right all along; it is that Jesus has promised, irrespective of my success or failure, to be there. He assures me not of my innocence but of my forgiveness and my hope. He was raised to life, says St Paul, for our justification; he was raised so that we may know his promise to be with us is never defeated by our failures.

We struggle with the dilemmas of our age; we do our best to test and challenge our own convictions, to bring them to the truth; but we know too that they will be shadowed with our own secret needs and frailties, that they will not simply be a clear witness to truth and goodness. We accept that, even as we work for good ends, we shall find ourselves wandering or compromised. We make our decisions about right and wrong, good and evil, as prayerfully and carefully as we can, and try to find the courage to take the consequences of those decisions. But we resolve not to see in each other absolute good or evil; we recognize that the denial of evil in ourselves does not help the cause of good. And so we follow Jesus, 'justified' by his gift of love alone. We pray and trust that he will, bit by bit, deliver us from evil, inside as well as outside. We turn our eyes away from the seductive image of a righteous, settled soul with nothing more to learn or to repent. We keep our eyes on Jesus and follow his gaze – towards the Father's heart. We stop clinging, stop demanding that God will serve our need to be in the right. We make our mistakes and we own them. We are justified by faith, as we resolve to follow the risen Jesus into the unknown depths of God's life; and if we can begin to live out such a faith in the resurrection, we shall, with Mary, prompt others to come and ponder the empty tomb and take the first steps on Jesus' path.

INTO DAYLIGHT

Easter Morning broadcast 2004

In a few minutes, we shall hear St Paul telling us why Easter matters to every one of us, and especially to everyone who makes the great decision to trust that what Jesus says is true and that what Jesus does makes all the difference. If you believe that Jesus rose from the dead, you are not just believing an odd fact from two thousand years ago; you are trusting that there is a kind of life, a kind of love and trust and joy that is the very essence of Jesus' identity which is now coming to life in you. And as it comes to life, you begin to know that no amount of pressure and stress and suffering in your life has power in itself to break the bond that has been created between you and Jesus' life and activity. You are alive with a fuller and deeper life than just your own. Your resources are more than you could ever have imagined.

Jesus rises from the dead so as to find not only his home in heaven but his home in us. He rises so that we may rise out of the prisons of guilt, anxiety, self-obsession or apathy that so constantly close around us. But for this to happen, says St Paul, we have to go on, day after day, getting used to parts of us dying, just as Jesus died: we have to get used to the beloved habits of self-serving and self-protecting being brought into the light that shines from Jesus' face and withering away in that brightness. That's why Paul says that Christians go around with both death and life at work in their lives – always trying to let the light of Jesus kill off these sick and deadly habits, always letting the new life that is ours but so much more than ours shine through.

This year, both the Eastern and the Western churches celebrate Easter on the same day. It doesn't happen all that often, and when it does it's a great opportunity for us in the West to remember what we owe to the insight and genius of Christians from the Greek and Syrian and Russian worlds. One of the most important contributions has been their vision of how the light of God in Jesus can inhabit this ordinary world and shine visibly in the faces of Christian people. In the art of the Eastern Church, in the great icons of Greece and Russia, we can see a sort of visual commentary on St Paul's words. Here are human figures seen against the background of divine light; and the light doesn't take away their human features but makes them transparent, stretches them and reshapes them in great elongated forms whose powerful flowing lines seem to speak of another world that has come to life in the middle of this one. Any of you who've seen the El Greco exhibition in London this spring will recognize that El Greco is doing just this; he was an artist who had been trained by Greek painters of icons, so it isn't surprising.

That's the visual expression of what Paul has to say about the Easter news of new life. Ordinary humanity, ordinary physical reality, your bodily life and mine are being transfigured from within by the presence of God's glory.

It was still dark, says St John as he begins his story of the rising of Jesus; and at the end of the passage he says that up to the point when the two disciples look into the empty tomb and see the folded grave-clothes they hadn't understood what the Jewish scriptures were all about. As they go back to join the others, the dawn begins to break; the light is rising in their minds and it's no longer dark.

St John uses this imagery again and again. In the very first chapter of his gospel, we read that the light has shone in the darkness and the darkness hasn't quenched it. When Judas Iscariot leaves the Last Supper to betray Jesus, John says that 'He went out; and it was night' (*John* 13.30). After the story we have just heard and the following story of Jesus' meeting with Mary Magdalene, we hear of Jesus coming to the other disciples in their locked room 'late in the evening'. Where Jesus is around, the view becomes clear; darkness is put to flight. And this is why our worship at Easter traditionally begins with the lighting of a fire and the blessing of a candle.

Jesus lights up the landscape; and what St John tells us here is that one bit of the landscape that he lights up is the Bible itself. The disciples haven't known how to read their own scriptures until now; but they come to see that the events of Good Friday are part of the pattern of God's work with his people all along. Salvation and renewal always come as people are shocked into the recognition of how deeply they have betrayed God. God is always faithful to his people, even when all they have to give him is rejection and contempt. And no human rejection can destroy

God's promise and God's longing to be with those he loves. This is what that first Easter morning begins to get across to them. Not even the torturing to death of Jesus can change this love; and so when the disciples come looking for a body, they find an empty grave – like a door open into God's future.

So, if we can turn one more time to the icons of the Eastern Church, it is fitting that we so often see Jesus in glory holding an open book. Sometimes it just carries the Greek letters Alpha and Omega, the first and last letters of the Greek alphabet; sometimes it has a specific text from the Bible. But the point is the same: all that is written in our book, the Bible, is what Jesus presents to us for our reading and understanding. If we don't follow his finger along the text, we read wrong. So our Bible isn't just a holy book we can open and consult for answers without any more ado; we need to try and read it in the presence and in the Spirit of Jesus, to see how all of it finds its unity around him and in relation to him, to what he says and does in his life and his death.

But of course it's the whole landscape of our life and our reality that is enlightened by Jesus. In this light we see who God really is, how deep his faithfulness is to us. We see who we are, how constantly we fail, but also how passionately we are loved and valued. We see each other, as people valued by God, and our attitudes are drastically changed. We see the material world itself full of God's glory, demanding our reverence and care.

So with the two disciples, we look this morning into the empty tomb as if through an open door. On the other side is a world drenched with light, God's beauty shining through; yet it's our own world we are seeing, seeing it as God made it to be, seeing ourselves as God made us to be. We are walking into daylight.

PRESENTE

Easter 2004

A good few years ago, I heard a distinguished American scholar of ancient history commenting on the proclamation of the resurrection as it would have been heard in the classical world. 'If an educated Greek or Roman had been told that someone had been raised from the dead,' he said, 'his first question would have been, "How do you get him back into his grave again?"' The point was that most of those who first heard the Easter gospel would have found it grotesque or even frightening. Resurrection was not a joyful sign of hope but an alarming oddity, something potentially very dangerous. The dead, if they survived at all, lived in their own world – a shadowy place, where they were condemned to a sort of half-life of yearning and sadness. So Vergil at least represents it in his great epic, unforgettably portraying the dead as 'stretching out their hands in longing for the other side of the river'. But for them to return would have been terrifying and unnatural; the boundaries between worlds had to be preserved and protected.

Even the ancient Hebrews, who first made resurrection a positive idea, thought of the condition of the dead in just such a way: and resurrection was something that would happen at the end of time, when the good would be raised to receive their reward and the wicked their punishment, as in the prophecy of Daniel. But the news that someone had been raised from the tomb *now* would have been as disturbing for the Jew as for the Greek, if not perhaps quite so straightforwardly frightening. When St Matthew tells us that between the death and the ascension of Jesus many holy people of older days left their tombs in Jerusalem and appeared to many in the city, he is portraying not a scene of happy reunion but a true earthquake in the established order of the universe. It all helps us make sense of that unmistakable element in the resurrection stories that speaks of terror and amazement.

But why might resurrection be such a problem? Apart from the total confusion of present and long-term future which resurrection involved for the Jew, and the untidy blurring of boundaries between worlds for the Greek, there is another factor. When the dead did appear in vision or dream in the ancient world, it was often to denounce their killers; and the ancient empires specialized in mass slaughter. What would it have meant to a Roman to be told not only that the dead could return but that the 'firstborn from the dead', the first fruits of the harvest, was one who had been among the victims of the empire's legal system? Ancient empires grew and survived by assuming that enormous quantities of human lives were expendable and unimportant; those who fell victim to the system simply disappeared. But what if they didn't? Here was a message that might well cause alarm: an executed criminal, instead of disappearing into oblivion, is brought back into the world and his friends are told to speak in his name to his killers, telling them that for their life and health they must trust that he has made peace for them with God.

And what was worse still was that this was seen not as an isolated matter: the risen one was only the first. His rising from death guaranteed that all would be raised, that no life would be forgotten and obliterated, or even relegated to the everlasting half-light of Hades. Death does not end relationships between human persons and between human persons and God; and this may be sobering news as well as joyful, sobering especially for an empire with blood on its hands. We forget so readily what Christianity brought into the world; we are so used to it that we think it is obvious. In the ancient world there was absolutely no assumption that every life was precious. Fathers had the right to kill their children in certain circumstances, masters their slaves; crowds flocked to see criminals or prisoners of war killing each other in the theatres; massacre was a normal tool of war. Some philosophers defended a theory of abstract human equality, but they were untroubled by the political facts of life in which lives were expendable in these familiar ways. It is a shock to realize just how deeply rooted such an attitude was. And when all is said and done about how Christianity has so often failed in its own vision, the bare fact is that it brought an irreversible shift in human culture. Human value could not be extinguished by violence or death; no-one could be forgotten.

The gospel of the resurrection announced many great things, but this must have been one of the most disturbing of all. Here and now, God holds on to the lives of all the departed – including the lives that have been wasted, violently cut short, damaged by oppression. All have worth in his sight. If God can raise as the messenger of his word and the giver of his life a man who has been through the dehumanizing process of a Roman state execution, a process carefully designed to humiliate and obliterate, then the imperial power may well begin to worry.

We don't live under an empire like that, thank God. Yet we look back on a century in which imperial powers have in so many ways sought to obliterate their victims, as if the resurrection never happened. At Auschwitz there is an inscription in Hebrew from the Old Testament, 'O earth, cover not their blood'; the Holocaust, along with the mass killings of the thirties in the Soviet Union or the revolutionary years in China, went forward at the hands of people who assumed as blandly as any ancient Roman that the dead could be buried once and for all and forgotten. Cambodia and Rwanda and the Balkans remind us that it doesn't need to be an imperial power; it may be your closest neighbours who turn into murderers.

Now we may not have that kind of blood on our hands; but there are times when we are convicted of sharing something of that assumption about the dead. Who is there who has not felt a little of this conviction, reading in these last few weeks the heart-breaking stories that mark the tenth anniversary of the genocide in Rwanda? It is not that we wielded the weapons; but the nations of the world stood by in indecision and distractedness while the slaughter went on. Some lives, it seems, are still forgettable; some deaths still obliterate memory, for those of us at a distance. And as I speak, the carnage in Northern Uganda continues; just a matter of weeks ago, a mass killing there failed to make anything like an adequately serious impact on great tracts of the media; and most people here are not aware of the nearly one million displaced persons in that region, living in continual fear, and the nightmare situation of the hundreds of thousands of children kidnapped to be soldiers, to kill and be killed. When deaths like this are forgotten, the gospel of the resurrection should come as a sharp word of judgement, as well as of hope.

But hope, of course, it is. We may and we should feel the reproach of the risen Christ as we recognize how easily we let ourselves forget; and nearer home, we might think too of those who die alone and unloved in our own society – the aged with no family (or forgotten by their family), the homeless addict, the mentally disturbed isolated from ordinary human contact. But Easter tells us to be glad that they are not forgotten by God, that their dignity is held and affirmed by God and that their lives are in his hand. In that gladness, we should be stirred to turn our eyes to look for those likeliest to be forgotten and to ask where our duty and service lies. God's justice rebukes our forgetfulness; and the truth that he will never let go of the lost and needy, so far from being an alibi for us not to bother, is a reminder of the responsibility of service and reverence laid upon all of us.

But the goodness of the resurrection news is most evident for those who have lost people they love to any sort of incomprehensible evil – the tragedies of dementia, the apparent meaning-lessness of accident, the horrors of violence or injustice. Think back for a moment to the days when death squads operated in countries like Argentina or El Salvador: the Christians there developed a very dramatic way of celebrating their faith, their hope and their resistance. At the liturgy, someone would read out the names of those killed or 'disappeared', and for each name someone would call out from the congregation,

Presente, 'Here'. When the assembly is gathered before God, the lost are indeed *presente*; when we pray at this Eucharist 'with angels and archangels and the whole company of heaven', we say *presente* of all those whom the world (including us) would forget and God remembers. With angels and archangels; with the butchered Rwandans of 10 years ago and the butchered or brutalized Ugandan children of last week or yesterday; with the young woman dead on a mattress in King's Cross after an overdose and the childless widower with Alzheimer's; with the thief crucified alongside Jesus and all the thousands of other anonymous thieves crucified in Judaea by an efficient imperial administration; with the whole company of heaven, those whom God receives in his mercy. And with Christ our Lord, the firstborn from the dead, by whose death our sinful forgetfulness and lukewarm love can be forgiven and kindled to life, who leaves no human soul in anonymity and oblivion, but gives to all the dignity of a name and a presence. He is risen; he is not here; he is present everywhere and to all. He is risen: *presente*.

THE DENIAL OF DEATH

Easter 2005

Death, says St Paul, is our enemy (*1 Corinthians* 15.26); and Christians are the most pitiable of all people if their hope is confined to this life. To many modern ears, these statements sound a bit suspect. Isn't this the kind of religion we have learned to be wary of, a religion that justifies suffering and frustration here and now by the promise of compensation somewhere else? And as for regarding death as an enemy – is this more than the childish resentment of human beings who haven't yet accepted their limitations? One of the great books of the twentieth century, by a man who had read Freud more intelligently than most, was called *The Denial of Death*, and it spelled out the evil consequences of this refusal to face our limits, the anxiety and unreality and psychological fragility that could distort lives lived in this state of denial.

The longing for everlasting life takes strange forms. There are people who obsessively investigate the evidence for spiritualist phenomena, people who have their bodies cryogenically frozen in the hope of resuscitation, people who claim that their diet and lifestyle is slowing down the ageing process. And of course when you think of things like this, you realize that it isn't simply certain kinds of religion that produce odd and unhealthy attitudes to ageing or limitation or death. Quite a lot of our contemporary culture is actually shot through with a resentment of limits and the passage of time, anger at what we can't do, fear or even disgust at growing old. Ernest Becker's book, referred to a moment ago, was directed not against religion as such but against a climate of fantasy encouraged by cheap psychology ('you can be anything you choose to be') and a childlike faith in technology.

Now St Paul doesn't show too many obvious signs of resenting human limitations or indeed wanting not to die – after all, he tells us in all kinds of ways in the course of his letters that we have to let our self-protective instincts 'die' as we grow into the full scope of love for God and each other; so he can hardly be recommending to us the kind of attitude that gave Freud and Nietzsche so much material for criticism. What then is he saying here? And how do we hear it now as good news?

The first thing to notice is something that has been said countless times, yet we still miss it. Paul does not say that we shall live for ever; he says that we shall die and that we shall be raised as Jesus was raised. Forget spiritualism and cryogenics; forget supposed evidence for 'survival'. Paul doesn't think we are going to survive but that we are going to live again because of God's action. Here and now, we must indeed come to terms with the reality of death, and we must put to death all in us that binds us to our narrow self-interest. Indeed, you could rightly say that Paul's teaching is really that we must put to death our refusal to die, because that refusal to die, that fearful denial of our limits, is the root of our selfish and self-paralyzing habits of sin. A healthy human environment is one in which we try to make sense of our limits, of the accidents that can always befall us, and the passage of time which inexorably changes us. An unhealthy environment is one in which we always look for someone to blame and someone to compensate us, and struggle to maintain fictions of our invulnerability to time and change.

Societies as well as individuals fall victim to these diseases. We react so often with panic and hostility to the presence of persons and cultures who are different and blame them for our own dysfunctions. We maintain a ludicrous confidence in technology to solve the environmental problems it has itself intensified because we can't believe that our capacity to generate wealth and comfort for ourselves is anything other than infinite. We fantasize about a state of security so complete that nothing and no-one will ever threaten us. We need to hear that all this is really the denial of death – that it is what Paul elsewhere calls 'the works of the flesh', the closing up of ourselves in the face of a reality we can't fully control.

What Paul is telling us is this. If your hope is that this life will be protected and prolonged, that your comfort zone as you understand it will never be challenged, that you will never have to face the reality of being mortal and limited, God help you. It's a recipe for illusion, terror and the killing of the soul. But that doesn't mean that your 'real' life only begins on the far side of death. Rather it means that here and now you learn to live not by self-defence but by opening up to what God gives.

Why? Because that is the essence of belief in the resurrection. It is not a matter of natural survival, not a right we can demand from God, but a gift. God has promised to be our God, he has promised to hold us in relationship with himself whatever happens to us. Remember the end of *Romans* chapter 8? 'There is nothing in death or life ... nothing in all creation that can separate us from the love of God in Christ Jesus our Lord.' He has committed himself to be there for us by his own gracious decision; we face death knowing that his promise has been given – but not knowing (as St Paul goes on to say) just how the promise will be honoured. All we can guess is that our present life has the same relation to the future as the seed has to the full-grown plant. Not survival, but growth into an unimaginably greater dimension. If we now begin to live in a way that gives priority to God's promise and gift, to live in trust and generosity, we shall not be haunted and imprisoned by fear of death. We have begun to live the kind of life that can cope with death because it simply looks for God's gift at every point.

So the importance of Jesus' resurrection is not that it somehow proves there is life after death in a general sort of way. What it proves is that God keeps his promises: the commitment of God the

Father to Jesus his beloved son is absolute and
eternal; so the cross does not separate Father
and Son, and life is restored on the far side
of the cross, life that both is and isn't like the
ordinary physical life Jesus had in Galilee. And
the divine promise Jesus, God among us, makes
to his friends, the promise of mercy and renewal,
is absolute; not even the unfaithfulness of the
disciples can destroy it. Jesus' life is there for
them once more, the source of their joy and
hope. The violent and terrible death of Jesus does
not stop God from giving what he wants to give,
giving consistently and steadily. If Jesus is raised,
we can count on the faithfulness of God.

And perhaps we can dimly see why death can be
called an enemy. Death seems to challenge the
idea of an eternally faithful God; and it poses an
obvious difficulty for any belief that God wants
to develop with us a relationship that is always
growing and developing. It looks as though death
means that our relation with God comes to a halt,
as if God eventually treats us as disposable. But
if we see in Jesus' resurrection the confirmation
that God is faithful, we can face death differently
– not because it has stopped mattering or even
hurting, not because we have assurance that we

shall carry on as before (we shan't), but because God has not finished with us. We have more to receive from him, and he will create the conditions that will make it possible for us to receive.

Death will be the last enemy to be overcome, says Paul. At the end of everything, death will be behind us, death will be history. We shall have become what we have become because we have lived with death and learned how to love realistically and humbly, within the compass of a limited life. Death the enemy of our confidence has been a friend to us after all – an enemy we learn to love, as Christ tells us to love our enemies; and at the end of everything its work is done. What remains is only growth in love, as we stand with and in Jesus Christ looking into the inexhaustible depths of God's reality – the sea we must learn to swim in but will never cross over, as the Welsh poet Ann Griffiths put it in one of her hymns.

And here and now we are called on to challenge the denial of death that locks us into folly and fear; the pride and arrogance, the desperation and brittleness of our hopes. Easter proclaims to individuals and economic systems and governments alike that we shall not find life by refusing to let go of our precious, protected selves. Let go with Christ, die into his love; and rise with Christ, opening yourself to the eternal gift of the Father.

Conspiracies and Transparencies

Easter 2006

One of the ways in which we now celebrate the great Christian festivals in our society is by a little flurry of newspaper articles and television programmes raking over the coals of controversies about the historical basis of faith. So it was no huge surprise to see a fair bit of coverage given a couple of weeks ago to the discovery of a 'Gospel of Judas', which was (naturally) going to shake the foundations of traditional belief by giving an alternative version of the story of the passion and resurrection. Never mind that this is a demonstrably late text which simply parallels a large number of quite well-known works from the more eccentric fringes of the early century Church; this is a scoop, the real, 'now it can be told' version of the origins of Christian faith.

You'll recognize the style, of course, from the saturation coverage of the Da Vinci Code literature. We are instantly fascinated by the suggestion of conspiracies and cover-ups; this has become so much the stuff of our imagination these days that it is only natural, it seems, to expect it when we turn to ancient texts, especially Biblical texts. We treat them as if they were unconvincing press releases from some official source, whose intention is to conceal the real story; and that real story waits for the intrepid investigator to uncover it and share it with the waiting world. Anything that looks like the official version is automatically suspect. Someone is trying to stop you finding out what really happened, because what really happened could upset or challenge the power of officialdom.

It all makes a good and characteristically 'modern' story – about resisting authority, bringing secrets to light, exposing corruption and deception; it evokes Watergate and *All the President's Men*. As someone remarked after a television programme about the Da Vinci Code, it's almost that we'd prefer to believe something like this instead of the prosaic reality. We have become so suspicious of the power of words and the way that power is exercised to defend those who fear to be criticized. The first assumption we make is that we're faced with spin of some kind, with an agenda being forced on us – like a magician forcing a card on the audience. So that the modern response to the proclamation 'Christ is risen!' is likely to be, 'Ah, but you would say that, wouldn't you? Now, what's the real agenda?'

We don't trust power; and because the Church has historically been part of one or another sort of establishment and has often stood very close to political power, perhaps we can hardly expect to be exempt from this general suspicion. But what it doesn't help us with is understanding what the New Testament writers are actually saying and why. We have, every Easter, to strip away the accumulated lumber of two thousand years of rather uneven Christian witness and try to let the event be present in its first, disturbing immediacy.

For the Church does not exist just to transmit a message across the centuries through a duly constituted hierarchy that arbitrarily lays down what people must believe; it exists so that people in this and every century may encounter Jesus of Nazareth as a living contemporary. This sacrament of Holy Communion that we gather to perform here is not the memorial of a dead leader, conducted by one of his duly authorized successors who controls access to his legacy; it is an event where we are invited to meet the living Jesus as surely as did his disciples on the first Easter Day. And the Bible is not the authorized code of a society managed by priests and preachers for their private purposes, but the set of human words through which the call of God is still uniquely immediate to human beings today, human words with divine energy behind them. Easter should be the moment to recover each year that sense of being contemporary with God's action in Jesus. Everything the church does – celebrating Holy Communion, reading the Bible, ordaining priests or bishops – is meant to be in the service of this contemporary encounter. It all ought to be transparent to Jesus, not holding back or veiling his presence.

Yes, the sceptic will say, all very well, but why on earth should I believe that? Especially when it comes from the mouth of a figure who clearly has a bit of a vested interest in getting me to believe it, or from an institution that doesn't always look like a model of transparency? Well, all any preacher can do is point to how the text of the New Testament actually works. Two points at least are worth bearing in mind. First, it was written by people who, by writing what they

146

did and believing what they did, were making themselves, in the world's terms, less powerful, not more. They were walking out into an unmapped territory, away from the safe places of political and religious influence, away from traditional Jewish religion and from Roman society and law. As the Gospels and Paul's letters and the difficult, enigmatic letter 'to the Hebrews' all agree, they were putting themselves in a place where they shared the humiliation experienced by condemned criminals going naked in public procession to their execution.

Second, the New Testament was written by people who were still trying to find a language that would catch up with a reality bigger than they had expected. The stories of the resurrection especially have all the characteristics of stories told by people who are struggling to find the right words for an unfamiliar experience – like the paradoxes and strained language of some of the mystics. The disciples really meet Jesus, as he always was, flesh and blood – yet at first they don't recognize him, and he's something more than just flesh and blood. At the moment of recognition, when bread is broken, when the wounds of crucifixion are displayed, he withdraws again, leaving us floundering for words. He gives authority and power to the disciples to proclaim his victory and to forgive sins in his name, yet he tells Peter that his future is one in which he will be trussed up and imprisoned and hustled away to death.

So the New Testament is not a collection of books with a single tight agenda that works on behalf of a powerful elite; it is the product of a community of people living at great risk and doing so because they sense themselves compelled by a mystery and presence that is completely authoritative for them – the presence of Jesus. They have been convinced that being in the company of Jesus is the way to become fully and effectively human. They are discovering how to live together without greed, fear and suspicion because of his company. They believe that they've been given the gift of showing the world what justice and mutual service and gratitude might look like in a world that is a very dangerous place because of our incapacity for these things. They take the risks because they believe they have been entrusted with a promise.

Whatever this is, it is not about cover-ups, not about the secret agenda of power; it may be

Archbishop Gero's altar cross, c. 960, Cologne Cathedral, Germany/
© Dombauarchiv Köln, Matz and Schenk.

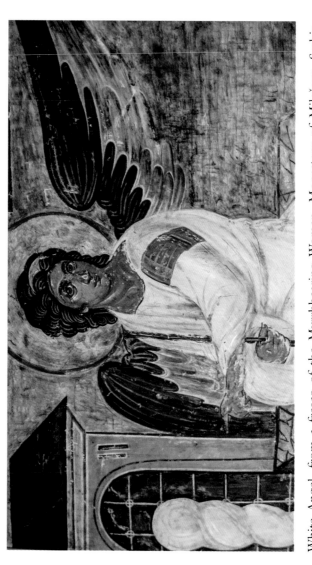

White Angel, from a fresco of the Myrrhbearing Women, Monastery of Mileševa, Serbia, c. 1235/by gracious permission of the Patriarch of Serbia and the Serbian Ministry of Culture.

nonsense to you, it may be unreal to you, but don't be deceived about the nature of the message and those who lived it out in the days when the New Testament was being written. And that's why, if we want to know what it is about today, we need to turn to the people who are taking the same risks, struggling with the same mystery. We need to look at the martyrs and the mystics. There are still those who tell us about God in Jesus Christ by lives of intense and mostly wordless prayer; how very powerfully God was to be seen in last year's extraordinary television series, 'The Monastery', where we saw some very ordinary human beings faced with the demands of a life in which you had to be truthful, where you had to be silent, where you had to search for reconciliation at all costs. But still more important, there are those who tell us about God in Jesus Christ by putting their lives at risk. There are places in our world where conversion to Christianity is literally a matter of putting your life on the line; we have all been following with agonized attention the story of Abdul Rahman in Afghanistan, and we know that his story is not unique. We can say there with absolute certainty that whatever the Gospel means in circumstances like that, it isn't a cover-up for the sake of the powerful.

149

But there are also places where what brings down the violence and the murderousness is simply a willingness to make reconciliation real. Nearly three years ago, during the bitter civil war in the Solomon Islands, a major part was played in peacemaking by the local Anglican religious order known as the Melanesian Brotherhood, a community of local men committed to a common discipline of praying and teaching and spreading the gospel as they travel round the villages, by drama and song and preaching. Seven of them were held hostage and killed in cold blood by a rebel group. The shock of that act of gratuitous butchery jolted almost everyone involved into beginning a peace process; the brothers continue to be involved at every level in that work.

Last summer, a number of the brothers visited England, taking their songs and their drama into churches and schools in a number of areas. Everyone who has seen them at work will remember it all their lives. One of the things they did was to perform a passion play; and this is what one of them wrote about it.

This passion was our own testimony to
our seven brothers who were murdered

in 2003. For Christ-like they became the innocent victims of the violence they had worked so hard to stop. They were beaten and mocked and tortured and recorded on tape recorders in the sickening mockery of a trial before their murderers … They were put to death for the sins of the people. And they live on. I wish I could show you these men and their goodness and their innocence. And when we see real evil we must recognize it too: the opposition, the true sin of our world where brutality of this nature becomes a cause to be justified.

… Our story of the Passion of Christ took place 2,000 years ago but it is still taking place throughout our world today. But we have been changed. We did not travel from the other side of the world to preach a death but to preach a resurrection. For we know where we stand and we know who we belong to. And we believe there is a choice in all this, a choice to belong to the life-giver.

'We know where we stand and we know who we belong to'. Beyond all the history of confusion and betrayal that surrounds a lot of the Church's history, beyond the power games that we still play in the churches, this one rock-like conviction remains, the conviction that drove the writing of every word of the New Testament. Nothing to do with conspiracies, with the agenda of the powerful; everything to do with how the powerless, praying, risking their lives for the sake of Christ and his peace, are the ones who understand the Word of God. And to accept that is not to sign up to the agenda of a troubled, fussy human society of worried prelates and squabbling factions. It is to choose life, to choose to belong to the life-giver.

LIBERATING TRUTH

Easter 2007

It was two and a half years ago; we had just finished a substantial open-air meal after a Eucharist on the football field in the tiny island of Malaita in the Solomons. The Premier of Malaita had been talking about the bloody civil war that had divided the islands until just a year earlier [see also the preceding sermon]; and then he said, 'I want you to bless us; I need to say in public that we were responsible as well as the people on the other islands. So I'm going to ask the crowd to be quiet, and then I'll kneel down and ask you to pronounce God's forgiveness for whatever we contributed to the horrors of these last years.'

Sometimes you know that you have heard the reality of the gospel as you've never heard it before. Here was a politician, representing a community that had suffered greatly and inflicted great suffering as well, simply saying, 'We were all wrong. We all needed healing and forgiveness. The problem isn't them but us – all of us, or us and them.' And it was as if for the first time you could see the bare bones of what reconciliation means.

There is a huge step from looking back over past history and telling only your story and looking back to find out what other stories there are and giving them room to be heard also. I don't know whether Ian Paisley and Gerry Adams, a few weeks back, were beginning to take that step, but at least they helped to make it possible for others. There have been two stories in Northern Ireland for such a long time, two incompatible stories – Catholics telling the story of heartless British imperialism, systematic discrimination and economic injustice, corrupt law enforcers; Protestants telling the story of heartless terrorism, religious authoritarianism, priests who secretly promote violence. And then there comes a moment when the possibility is just dimly discerned that neither of these perceptions is an objective record; that everyone in this history made decisions, some shockingly evil, some tragic, some foolish – and that those decisions and the sufferings that came from them don't have the power to tell you what decisions you have to make today.

Our natural human default setting, when we're stuck in conflict, seems to be to ask those around to agree with us that our story is the right one, and that no amount of suffering or tragedy on the other side can compare with ours. And if you suggest that they might need listening to as well, you are regarded as in effect justifying the terrible things they have done. We do it in our individual relationships, as all of us here will know. And we do it, compulsively and destructively, in the relationships between nations and cultures, demanding that the world recognize our exclusive claim to innocence.

Now there are relationships in which the imbalance is enormous – we've recently been recalling one such in the shape of the grim history of slavery. There are hideously abusive relationships between individuals, marriages scarred with horrific violence for example, or the abuse of children. No sane person will pretend that everyone is equally to blame.

But the point is that the situation is not changed by someone being declared completely innocent, and someone else completely guilty. What changes things is seeing that the horror of violence against a child or against an enslaved race is dreadful not just because the victim is innocent but because the victim is human and helpless. The shared story is not a cartoonishly simple tale of absolute embodied evil and absolute embodied innocence, but a human story of pain, error, violence and sin, a vortex into which people have been drawn, innocently or not so innocently. And in relation-ships between persons or groups more or less equal and grown-up, going forward requires us all to learn a measure of openness to discovering things about ourselves we did not know, seeing ourselves through the eyes of another. What they see may be fair or unfair, but it is a reality that has been driving someone's reactions and decisions. We'd better listen, hateful and humili-ating though it may be for some of us.

Now what the events of Good Friday and Easter tell us is that every single human being is impli-cated in something profoundly wrong. We say, rather glibly, that Jesus died for our sins, that he died to save humankind – and thereby we say that we are all in need of something we cannot find or manufacture for ourselves, in need of a word, a gift, a touch from someone else, somewhere else, so that we can be made free of whatever it is that keeps us in the clutch of illusions and failures. If the purpose of Jesus dying was that all might be made whole, the implication is that all have been sick. So that Good Friday tells all of us, those who think they're good and those who know they're bad, all alike, to look inside and ask what part we would have played in the drama of the Lord's death. There is only one innocent character in that drama and it isn't me or you. So for all of us there is something in our lives that would, if it came to it, if it reigned unchecked in us, allow us to range ourselves with the crucifiers – some habit of selfishness or fear, some prejudice, some guilt that we don't want confronted, some deficit in love or lovability. In some way, however small, we have already contributed to the death of Jesus. He is there on the cross because we are the way we are.

But on Easter Day, this bleak recognition is turned on its head. We were all involved; yet the combined weight of every human failure and wrongness, however small or great, all of that could not extinguish the creative love of God. We share one human story in which we are all caught up in one sad tangle of selfishness and fear and so on. But God has entered that human

story; he has lived a life of divine and unconditional love in a human life of flesh and blood. He
has not protected himself, or forced anyone to
accept him. And in this world that human beings
have made for themselves, this world of politics
and religion and social cooperation, divine love
loses. It is helpless to maintain itself in the face of
the so-called real world. The vortex of error and
failure that affects everybody in the world draws
Jesus into its darkness and seems to destroy him
body and soul. That, says Good Friday, is the
kind of world this is, and we are all part of it.

Yet there is more than the world to think about. If
that love is really what it claims to be, eternal and
unconditional, it will not be destroyed. What's
more, the human embodiment of that love, the
flesh and blood of Jesus, cannot be destroyed. As
we heard in the reading from *Acts* this morning,
the friends of Jesus ate and drank with him after
he was raised from the dead – as we are doing in
this Holy Communion (*Acts* 10.34–43, esp. 41).
The life that God brought into the world in Jesus
is here forever with us.

So if we can accept the unwelcome picture of us,
and our world, that Good Friday offers, we are,

in the strangest way, set free to hear what Easter says. Give up the struggle to be innocent and the hope that God will proclaim that you were right and everyone else wrong. Simply ask for whatever healing it is that you need, whatever grace and hope you need to be free, then step towards your neighbour; Easter reveals a God who is ready to give you that grace and to walk with you. In St Paul's bold words in his letter to the Roman Christians (*Romans* 11.32), 'In making all mankind prisoners to disobedience, God's purpose was to show mercy to all mankind.'

When in our world we are faced with the terrible deadlocks of mutual hatred and suspicion, with rival stories of suffering and atrocity, we have to pray for this resurrection message to be heard. In the Middle East, in Northern Ireland and the Balkans and Sri Lanka, in the tribal conflicts of Africa, in the suspicions between Muslims who associate all Christians with the Crusaders and Christians who associate all Muslims with terrorism, in our most tangled and unhappy personal relations, and yes, in the bitter conflicts in the Church too – can we take in what Good Friday and Easter Day have to say to us? That we are all trapped, and we shall only come out of the traps we have made for ourselves when we grasp that God is greater than we are and is determined to go on living his life among us whatever happens? If so, we are free, like that extraordinary politician on Malaita, to face the past with courage and realism and to begin the risky journey towards true reconciliation.

Swallowed Up in Victory

Easter 2008

> The last enemy to be overcome is death
> (*1 Corinthians* 15.26)

Your hair and your nails may keep growing for a while after you die, but nothing else does. Death is when growing stops – the routine ways in which your body repairs itself and grows fresh tissue, and the ways in which the mind and heart stop developing. We know the suffering that is caused when the mind and heart have already apparently stopped responding even before physical death – the agonizing spectacle of vegetative states or dementia. That's why people sometimes speak of these conditions as death-in-life. Signs of life are signs of response and development, and when they're not obviously there, we don't know what sort of life is really present.

So too we talk of the death of a relationship when nothing moves it forward; and we say that individuals or whole cultures are in some sense dead when they seem to be producing nothing fresh; they've lost the skill of responding and can only repeat, like the unhappy person suffering from some sorts of dementia. We fear dementia because we fear being trapped in sameness, repetition; we fear the death of love and imagination; we fear death itself because it is the end of all change. And we know that it is inescapable.

Recognizing that this is so, that all the processes we value because they enlarge and enrich us will one day simply stop, is hard, but it is part of growing up. Artists, scientists and psychoanalysts have in different ways warned against the dangerous illusion of thinking we are immortal. Maturity lies in accepting the truth – and then making the most of every moment of sensation so that our response is as deep and wholehearted as may be.

> This thou perceiv'st, which makes thy
> love more strong,
> To love that well, which thou must leave
> ere long.

as Shakespeare has it at the end of one of his most memorable sonnets (no. 73).

Yet here comes the Easter gospel, apparently determined to upset this stoic maturity and to promise us just that eternal life we are urged to leave behind as a childish fantasy. Death will be 'overcome', 'swallowed up in victory' (*1 Corinthians* 15.54). Is the Christian gospel just a version of that popular but problematic passage sometimes read at funerals, beginning 'Death is nothing at all' and talking of it as just 'slipping into the next room'?

That's not quite the tone of what St Paul or any of the other New Testament writers is saying – nor of some of the ancient hymns and prayers of the Church in this season (nor even of the author of the sermon from which that passage is taken). 'Death and life have contended in that combat stupendous', says one early mediaeval hymn (the Sequence of Easter Sunday); and the whole idea of a battle between life and death in the events of Christ's death and resurrection doesn't suggest an event that is 'nothing at all'. Death takes quite bit of overcoming; there's a struggle involved here. And Jesus as he faces death seems to take it with utter seriousness, acknowledging terror and shrinking from it in his desperate prayer in Gethsemane. Easter may tell us that death is conquered, but it doesn't tell us that there was never any contest.

163

Perhaps that's the clue. Easter is not about denying death, and the resurrection doesn't make the nightmare death on the cross unreal. Death is exactly what the artists and scientists and psycho-analysts say: it is a full stop to human growth and response, it is night falling on everything we value or understand or hope for. Fear is natural, and so is grief at the death of another (Jesus, remember, shed tears for the death of a friend). Don't attempt to avoid it or deny its seriousness. On the contrary, keep it in view; remind yourself of it. When the tradition of the Church proposes that you think daily about death and prepare for it, it isn't being morbid but realistic: get used to it and learn to live with the fear. And meanwhile – Shakespeare was being entirely Christian in this respect – get used to loving and valuing things and persons irrespective of the fact that they won't be there for ever. Love them now, and what you would want to do for them, do now. 'Night is coming when no-one can work', says Jesus (*John* 9.4).

So what does it mean to say that, despite all this, death is 'defeated'? When death happens and growing stops, there are no more plans, no more hope of control: for the believer, there is only God left. Just as at the very beginning of creation, there is God, and there is the possibility that God has brought into being by his loving will. When death has done all it can do, God remains untouched and his will is the loving and generating will that it eternally is. When we look at death, we look at something that can destroy anything in our universe – but not God, its maker and redeemer. And if we accept that we shall die and all our hopes and schemes fall into the dark, we do so knowing that God is unchanged. So to die is to fall into the hands of the living God.

That is why the effort to keep death daily before us is a source of life and hope. It is to commend ourselves every day into God's hands, trusting that he is eternally a loving creator, in whom there is no darkness at all, as the New Testament says (*1 John* 1.5). And when we let ourselves go into God's hands, we do so confident that he is free to do what he wills with us – and that what he wills for us is life. The Easter story is not about how Jesus survived death or how the spirit of Jesus outlasted his mortal frame or whatever; it is about a person going down into darkness and the dissolving of all things and being called again out of that nothingness. Easter Day, as so many have said, is the first day of creation all over again – or, as some have put it, the eighth day of the week, the unimaginable extra that is assured by the fact that God's creative word is never stifled or silenced.

Celebrating Easter is celebrating the creator – celebrating the God whose self-giving purpose is never cancelled and who is always free to go on giving himself to those he has called. And resurrection for us is that renewed call: when we have fallen silent, when we no longer have any freedom to respond or develop, God's word comes to us again and we live (*2 Corinthians* 5.17). We can't really imagine it; it isn't just a continuation of our present life in slightly different circumstances but a new world. Yet all that God has seen and worked with in this life is brought into his presence once more and he renews his relationship with it all, spirit and body.

That is the overcoming of death – made clear to us in the only way it could be made clear, by the historical, tangible recreation of the life of Jesus, still recognizably who he always was, yet changed in ways we can't grasp in their fullness. Death is allowed to do its worst in him – not only in the form of physical pain and final extinction, but in the terror and desolation with which Jesus approaches it. He lets go of everything, even the hope that God will intervene to spare him. He descends into hell, and is brought up again by the creative call of his Father. A true struggle, an *agon* as the Greeks said, an agony of conflict; and a victory – not a reversal or cancellation but a new thing, risen life, the new age begun.

And so when we proclaim all this today, we as Christians are charged to address ourselves to two different sorts of delusion. On the one hand: we face a culture in which the thought of death is too painful to manage. Individuals live in anxious and acquisitive ways, seizing what they can to provide a security that is bound to dissolve, because they are going to die. Societies or nations do the same. Whether it is the individual grabbing the things of this world in just the repetitive, frustrating sameness that we have seen to be already in fact the mark of an inner deadness, or the greed of societies that assume there will always be enough to meet their desires – enough oil, enough power, enough territory – the same fantasy is at work. We shan't really die – we as individuals can't contemplate an end to our acquiring, and we as a culture can't imagine that this civilization like all others will collapse and that what we take for granted about our comforts and luxuries simply can't be sustained indefinitely. To all this, the Church says, sombrely, don't be deceived: night must fall.

On the other hand, this alone would only be to echo the not very helpful remark of John Maynard Keynes – 'In the long run, we are all dead'; not much of an Easter message! So the Church says: 'We shall die, we shall have no choice but to let go of all we cling to, but God remains. God's unshakeable love is untouched by death, and all we do and all we care about matters to him. He and he alone is free to make us afresh, to re-establish the world on the far side of every catastrophe.'

It isn't so much that Christians say, 'Death is not the end'. In an important sense, it *is* the end, and we must prepare for it as people of faith by daily seeking to let go of selfish, controlling, greedy habits, so that our naked souls are left face-to-face with the creating God. If we are prepared to accept in trust what Jesus proclaims, we can ask God for courage to embark on this path. We don't hope for survival but for re-creation – because God is who he is, who he has shown himself to be in Jesus Christ.

The vital significance of the Church in this society, in any human society, is its twofold challenge – first, challenging human reluctance to accept death, and then challenging any human acceptance of death without hope, of death as the end of all meaning. Death is real; death is overcome. We are mortal, and that is basic to who and what we are as humans. But equally we are creatures made so as to hear the call of God, a call that no power in heaven or earth can silence. That conviction is the foundation of all we say about human dignities and rights, and it is the heart of our Easter hope. The gospel, by insisting on both our limits and our eternal hope in God, safeguards equally the humility and realism we need for mature human life and the sense of a glory embodied in our mortality because it has been touched by God. Death is real; death is overcome. On that basis we claim to have a word to speak to our world that can renew every corner, every aspect, of our humanity.

THE HIDDEN SEED OF GLORY

Easter 2009

'Do you *know* that God exists?', the interviewers ask; or, 'How do you know Christian faith is true?' There are two tempting ways of responding, both wrong. There is the apologetic shuffle of saying, 'Of course, I don't really *know*; this is just the truth as it appears to me and I may be wrong.' And there is the confident offer to prove it all to the hearer's satisfaction; here are the philosophical arguments, here is the historical evidence, now what's the problem?

Two kinds of mistake: the first because it reduces faith to opinion and shrinks the scale of what you're trying to talk about to the dimensions of your own mind and preferences; the second because it keeps you at arm's length from the whole business by making it impersonal: here are the proofs and it doesn't much matter what I or anyone may be doing about it. It's just true in much the same way as it's true that Ben Nevis is the highest mountain in the British Isles. You may say, 'Well, there you go', but are unlikely to fall to your knees.

St Paul in today's epistle makes it clear that to speak of Jesus' resurrection is also to say something crucial about who and where we are, not just to make a claim about the past. Now we should not doubt for a moment that Paul means what he says and that he takes for granted that the resurrection of Jesus is not a piece of fantasy or wishful thinking but the actual emptying of a grave. However, the point of Paul's entire teaching on the resurrection is to take us much further than that. This event, the emptying of the grave, has done something and has brought the Christians of Colossae – like all Christians – into a new universe (*Colossians* 1.17–22). They are living in a new climate, with new 'thoughts' – a climate in which the various ways in which we've put up barriers between ourselves and God have been shattered and our old selves are dead. We may still go on trying to put those barriers back up again, but something has happened that opens up a new kind of future. Our selfish and destructive acts and reactions can be dealt with, overwhelmed again and again by the love shown in the cross of Jesus. Because of Jesus' death and rising from the dead, *our* resurrection has started, and our citizenship in heaven has begun. There is a hidden seed of glory within us, gradually coming to its fullness.

Resurrection has started. How do we know? Not by working it out and adopting it as well-founded opinion, not by deciding that this idea suits us, not by getting all the arguments straight, but because we are dimly aware of something having changed around us. For Paul's converts in Colossae, Corinth, or wherever, it's about the impact on them of his early visits: here was someone who, although he wasn't a good speaker or a charismatic teacher (so he himself tells us), was so intensely aware that the world had changed that he changed the world for those around him. They trusted him; they were prepared to risk all the mockery and harassment and worse that Christians had to put up with because they were able to say, 'It's so real for him that we can sense the sort of imperative urgency in what he says and what he sees; whatever he believes, this is life at a new level.'

That's why the two sorts of defence of faith I mentioned earlier aren't good enough. It's not that this is an attractive theory that I've decided to try out – but I may be wrong. Nor is it that I now have a knock-down argument that will convince everyone. There is something *compelling* here. I can't help being drawn to this promise of life and freedom. It isn't about my opinions only; yet I know that I can't put this into neat words that will make everyone say, 'Oh yes, it's obvious really'.

For a great many people, the burning question about faith is not just 'Can anyone believe this?' but 'Can anyone live like this?' Is it possible to live 'in heaven', in such a way that our selfishness is eroded? To live on the basic assumption that people can be healed of their miserable compulsions to fear and resent each other and to cling to their grievances and injuries? Last weekend's television drama, 'Five Minutes of Heaven', was a painfully sensitive reflection on what it takes to make reconciliation more than words alone, when a former terrorist gunman meets the brother of the man he killed in cold blood. Both, it turns out, are still locked into that past event: the gunman, though he has now become a sought-after speaker on reconciliation, is still trapped in self-loathing; the victim's brother, who witnessed the shooting as a boy of ten, is equally trapped, traumatized by what he saw as a child, helpless with rage that his brother's murderer has been 'forgiven' by a society with a short memory. When they meet at last, it is in an explosion of near-murderous violence; yet something is released, some future is opened.

'Five Minutes of Heaven': we're left in no doubt that *if* real reconciliation were possible, that would be what it was, five minutes of something quite other than the expectations and routines of this tragic world. And we're left in no doubt that getting there might be the most painful thing imaginable. The drama spared us nothing; but it did – courageously – suggest that 'heaven' was not an illusion. Can anyone live like that? Well, perhaps, perhaps just getting to the outer edge of something 'outside' the endless weary exchange of retaliation. A fleeting image of what Paul is talking about: another world that has taken root in this one – only not just through the chance experiences of a few individuals but because something has happened once and for all to declare that sin has been dealt with, the prison of the self has been broken open by God. The impossible is now possible. 'Your life is hidden with Christ in God' (*Colossians* 3.3), and you live from a depth newly opened up in you.

And the only way of saying that, of course, is for it to be lived out. It's no use talking endlessly – preaching endlessly – about reconciliation and forgiveness and liberation. No argument can persuade anyone about this, only the lived reality. It's worth remembering that Paul of Tarsus joined the Christian community not as a well-meaning religious enquirer but as someone who had been the equivalent of a terrorist gunman, someone who had supervised the activities of a private militia devoted to abducting and imprisoning members of the Christian sect. He is a perfectly intelligible figure in the back streets of modern Beirut or Baghdad. And he has to find his 'heaven' by going, undefended and unvouched for, to the people he has been trying to silence and kill. Can anyone live like this? If the Christians of Colossae or Corinth or Philippi had asked this, at least Paul would have been able to say 'Yes: I have lived it', or, 'It has lived itself out in me and in those who were my victims'. No wonder that he goes back over this so many times in his writings, and, in his second letter to Corinth, angrily protests that, whatever else may be true, he is not doing this for the sake of his comfort or power. Why should the Corinthians trust him (especially when there are more attractive teachers around)? Well, at least he has lived through the most appallingly painful realities of the reconciliation that Jesus made possible; he has lost an entire career, an entire identity, he has put his life at daily risk. The one thing the Corinthians can be sure of is that this is not an opinion or an argument.

And the moral of all this? It's boringly familiar. If we want to commend our faith, we have to show the difference. The new world has to be visible. In the days of the early church, writers trying to defend the faith naturally used all sorts of complex intellectual arguments; but they also said, 'Look at us. We try to live forgivingly with each other. We don't try to get revenge when we're killed by the state authorities or the lynch mobs. We treat every life as precious, including the lives you don't care about. We try to be peaceful and faithful, in private and in public, and to live lives of sexual faithfulness and self-control (as much of a challenge, we might add, in the late Roman Empire as it is today). Does all this suggest to you that there might be another way of living that offers healing to the casualties of so-called ordinary human behaviour?'

177

Early Christians could point to the martyrs – but also to those who freely decided to live lives of continence and poverty in the first monastic communities, the men and women who tried to live out the life of heaven in the daily discipline of life together, giving themselves time to discover their most deeply hidden failings and fears, their most deep-seated difficulties with themselves and other people and not running away but letting the action of God through the life of the community heal them bit by bit. We're still fascinated by this life – we joke about it, yet have an uneasy respect for it, as a whole series of television presentations will confirm. But there is a real question here to the Church, not least to the Church of England. More people than perhaps ever before want to have access to what the monastic life promises, the wisdom of mutual patience, shared silence and prayer, space to grow out of childish ways – yet the profile of monastic communities and the recognition given to those who seek the path of contemplation is pretty meagre. Is it time to pray for and work for a radical new affirmation of this life and a proper valuation of its gift to the Church and the world? To pray harder for vocations to this life and to encourage people of all ages to explore it and to have the courage to take those costly promises so as to begin to show the world what difference the faith makes – what the resurrection looks like?

It could hardly be a more propitious time for this. The present financial crisis has dealt a heavy blow to the idea that human fulfilment can be thought about just in terms of material growth and possession. Accepting voluntary limitation to your acquisitiveness, your sexual appetite, your freedom of choice doesn't look so absurd after all as a path to some sort of stability and mutual care. We should be challenging ourselves and our Church to a new willingness to help this witness to flourish and develop.

But it is of course only one form of witness. When all's said and done, the call is to every one of us. We need to hear what is so often the question that's *really* being asked when people say, 'How do you know?' And perhaps the only response that is fully adequate, fully in tune with the biblical witness to the resurrection, is to say simply, 'Are you hungry? Here is food.'

SHOWING SIGNS OF LIFE

Easter 2010

> God has appointed him to judge
> everyone, alive or dead. (*Acts* 10.41)

With a bit of a sigh, we read about yet another
legal wrangle over the right to wear a cross in
public while engaged in professional duties; one
more small but significant mark of what many
Christians feel is a sustained effort to discriminate
against them and render their faith invisible and
impotent in the public sphere. One more mark of
the curious contemporary belief that Christians
are both too unimportant for their convictions to
be worth bothering with and too dangerous for
them to be allowed to manifest those convictions.

Now it is quite likely that this latest folly, like
others, is less a sign of deep anti-Christian feeling
as such than the result of wooden-headed bureaucratic silliness combined with a well-meaning
and completely misplaced anxiety about giving
offence to non-Christians. But, while the legal
issues are being fought over and the exact scope

of religious freedom in the terms of human rights legislation is debated, we might step back a pace or two and think about the larger picture.

It is not the case that Christians are at risk of their lives or liberties in this country simply for being Christians. Whenever you hear overheated language about this, remember those many, many places where persecution is real and Christians are being killed regularly and mercilessly or imprisoned and harassed for their resistance to injustice. Remember our brothers and sisters in Nigeria and in Iraq, the Christian communities of southern Sudan fearing the outbreak of another civil war, the Christian minorities in the Holy Land facing the extinction of their two-thousand-year-old presence there; or our own Anglican friends in Zimbabwe, still – as I reminded this Cathedral congregation at Christmas – subject to routine attack from the security forces and locked out of their churches. That's not our situation, thank God, and we need to keep a sense of perspective, and to redouble our prayers and concrete support.

But we have a problem alright, and it needs reflection. Why this strange mixture of contempt and fear towards the Christian faith? If you think of all the high-profile attacks on Christianity that have been published in recent years, you may wonder why those who shout most loudly about the irreversible decline of Christianity campaign so ferociously against something which, on their own account, is withering away.

Some would answer that Christianity – in the shape of the Church of England anyway – still has a social and moral influence way beyond what its numbers justify; hence the campaigning. They see the Church as a retrograde force constantly seeking to impose alien standards on society, yet commanding very little grass roots support.

This doesn't quite wash. On many of the major moral questions of the day, the Christian Church still speaks for a substantial percentage of the country – not to mention speaking with the same concerns as people of other faiths. On burning questions like the rightness of assisted suicide, it is far from the case that the Christian view is only that of a tiny religious minority; and the debate is still very much alive. More important still is the very large number of the population who believe that Christian perspectives should have a place in

183

public discussion and decision-making – a belief that has been rather strengthened than otherwise by the realization in the last 18 months that the value-free climate of much of our financial and public life has poisoned and wounded our society more deeply than we knew. And at local level, the Church's continuing contribution to tackling the human problems no-one else is prepared to take on is one of the great untold stories of our time. I think of the work of a parish I visited in Cleethorpes a few weeks ago and the work they sponsor and organize with teenagers excluded from school in an area of high deprivation. I should be more impressed with secularist assaults if there were more sign of grass roots volunteer work of this intensity done by non-religious or anti-religious groups.

So yes, it's possible to understand the fear that religious people will automatically want to put the clock back to an age when the Church simply decided the fate of everyone and blandly appealed to supernatural authority when challenged. No-one, to coin a phrase, expects the Spanish Inquisition. There are things to be properly afraid of in religious history, Christian and non-Christian; there are contemporary religious philosophies of the Taliban variety which we rightly want to resist as firmly as we can. But we do need to say to some of our critics that a visit to projects like the one I have mentioned ought to make it plain enough that the last thing in view is some kind of religious tyranny. And if any of the Church's vocal critics would care to accompany me on such a visit, I should be delighted to oblige.

But the New Testament suggests there may be something more at work when people fear the gospel and the cross. Our second reading today hints at this (*Acts* 10.34–43). As so often in these early chapters of the *Acts of the Apostles*, St Peter underlines the fact that the resurrection of Jesus means that the one who was so decisively, annihilatingly, dismissed by the religious and political establishment of the time is the one who will decide the destiny of every human being. We shall all be judged by our response to him, to the divine and human person who has carried the cost of our mindless violence, our pride and self-satisfaction, our reluctance to face the truth. The court of final appeal in all human affairs is Christ; how we define ourselves in relation to him is a matter of life or death.

This is not about some fussy insistence on saying the right words and joining the right organization, as if St Peter were simply recruiting members for the Christian club. Jesus himself reminds us starkly in the gospel that we may be seeing him where we think we can't see him or don't know him – and that we may be failing to see him when we're making all the right noises about him. One day we are all going to discover in the presence of God who we are and how we stand with God, whether we can bear the presence of God for eternity; and in that moment of discovery, what will be crucial is how we have reacted to and understood the gift of God in the life and death of a man rejected and tortured to death.

The preaching of Peter and Paul and all the witnesses of the risen Jesus says that two basic things are demanded of us. First: we must acknowledge our own share in what the cross is and represents; we must learn to see ourselves as caught up in a world where the innocent are scapegoated and killed and where we are all unwilling, to a greater or lesser degree, to face unwelcome truths about ourselves. We must learn to see that we cannot by our own wisdom and strength cut ourselves loose from the tangle of injustice, resentment, fear and prejudice that traps the human family in conflict and misery.

And second: we must learn to trust that love and justice are not defeated by our failure; that God has provided from his own strength and resourcefulness a way to freedom, once we have become able to recognize in the face of the suffering Jesus his own divine promise of mercy and life. The resurrection is the manifesting to the world of the triumph of a love that uses no coercion or manipulation but is simply itself – an indestructible love. The challenge of Easter is to believe that God is not defeated by the most extreme rejection imaginable.

Good news? Emphatically yes. But not *easy* news. To recognize God in the crucified Jesus alters so much: it alters what we think about God, and it alters where we look for God in the human world. It suggests uncomfortably that God is likeliest to be found among those we have, like the religious and political establishment of Jesus' day, dismissed or shut out; it suggests that our models of success and failure have to be turned upside down; it suggests that our eternal future is bound up with whether we are able to turn to those we have hurt and seek forgiveness.

And so much else. Put like that, it is not surprising that the gospel and the cross could provoke fear and an unwillingness to allow such thoughts to become part of the current of public discussion. And perhaps it is not surprising either that we who call ourselves Christians may secretly be happier treating the cross just as a 'religious symbol' than letting ourselves be shaken and unmade and remade by it.

I don't imagine for a moment that much, if any, of this is going on in the mind of some hyper-conscientious administrative officer rebuking an employee for wearing a cross to work or even saying a prayer with a colleague. But perhaps we should take the opportunity of saying, 'This is what the cross actually means. If you want it to be invisible because it's too upsetting to people's security, I can well understand that; but let's have it out in the open. Is the God we see in the cross, the God who lives through and beyond terrible dereliction and death and still promises mercy, renewal, life – is that God too much of a menace to be mentioned or shown in the public life and the human interactions of society?'

For Christians, making the cross invisible is danger-
ously close to making both ultimate tragedy and
undefeated love invisible. If we fear what these petty
bureaucratic assaults mean, it should not be because
we fear for ourselves or our faith – or our God,
who is amply able to look after himself. It should
be because we fear for a society that cannot cope
with the realities of unspeakable human tragedy
and cannot cope, either, with the hope of ultimate
healing and reconciliation; a society that shrinks
into its comfort zones when challenged. At the
most extreme points, the defence of those comfort
zones can and often has meant the violent rejection
of Christian faith; we have lately been recalling
the martyrdom 30 years ago of Archbishop Oscar
Romero for his fearless rebukes to a murderous and
corrupt government in El Salvador. As I've said, we
must not dramatize our own situation unduly when
we see how serious the rejection of the cross *can*
be in circumstances like that. But there are connections – because the word of the cross, as St Paul said
(*1 Corinthians* 1.18), is a nonsense and a shock for
all who want to decide right and wrong, life and
death, only in terms of their own security.

So at least the petty annoyances of our context
may give us a chance to explain both why you

would be right to be afraid of the word of the cross and why you need to hear the risen Jesus saying '*Don't* be afraid!' The human condition is more serious and more terribly damaged than anyone wants to hear; but the resource of God's self-emptying love is greater than we have words to express. We are to be judged by our relation with the crucified; yet once we have accepted what that means, we are also released and absolved. If that is indeed the promise of the cross, it's well worth being obstinate about the freedom to show it to the world – so long as we ourselves are ready to show it in lives that look for Christ in the outcast, that examine their own failures in truthfulness and that constantly seek to share forgiveness and hope.

HAPPINESS OR JOY?

Easter 2011

We're now officially told that it's a good idea to be happy. Politicians have started talking about happiness rather than just prosperity, and there is even a research programme on the subject, trying to identify the essence of human well-being. And it's entirely appropriate that we are being encouraged to some public displays of shared celebration next Friday: let a thousand street parties blossom!

Now it's certainly a good thing that people have publicly acknowledged that there is more to life than the level of our Gross National Product, that we're just beginning to say out loud that corporate prosperity divorced from personal and communal fulfilment or stability is an empty thing. It's when we try and put more flesh on this that it becomes more complicated – and, worse still, more self-conscious. Some of you might just remember an episode of Doctor Who a couple of decades ago called 'The Happiness Patrol', where the Doctor arrives on a planet in which unhappiness is a capital crime, and blues musicians lead a dangerous underground existence. But less dramatically, most of us know the horrible experience of a family outing where things aren't going too well and Mum or Dad keeps saying, through ever more tightly gritted teeth, 'This is fun, isn't it?'

There's the catch: the deepest happiness is something that has crept up on us when we weren't looking. We can look back and say 'Yes, I was happy then' – and we can't reproduce it. It seems that, just as we can't find fulfilment in just loving ourselves, so we can't just generate happiness for ourselves. It comes from outside, from relationships, environment, the unexpected stimulus of beauty – but not from any programme that we can identify. It's a perfectly good idea to test and tabulate the ways people measure their own happiness – but beware of thinking that it will yield a foolproof method for being happy.

We have just heard the beginning of the resurrection story – a narrative of shock and amazement, utter disorientation (*John* 20.1–10). One of the things that makes these stories so believable is just that sense of unexpectedness

– the disciples don't come to the empty tomb and say, 'Well, there you are; just like he said.' They arrive never having really believed that their Lord would return from death, and now they find themselves in a disturbing new world where anything is possible; and so bright is the light in this new morning that even the familiar face of Jesus becomes unrecognizable. But as the story goes on in John's gospel, we are told that the disciples anxiously gathered in their locked room were 'filled with joy' when they saw Jesus among them. They have been jolted out of the rut of what is usual and predictable – and joy springs on them without warning, 'Christ the Tiger', in T. S. Eliot's great image.

What was it like for those first few hours after the empty tomb had been found, after Mary Magdalene had delivered her breathless message? It must have been a period of alarming uncertainty, half hope, half terror; which of us would really rejoice at the prospect of a miracle that would make us rethink most of what we had taken for granted? But into that chaos steps a figure before whose face 'the questions fade away' – the words with which C. S. Lewis finishes his greatest book, *Till We Have Faces*. And joy arrives, irresistibly. The world is even more dangerous and strange than before, the future is now quite unimaginable; but there is nothing that can alter the sheer effect of that presence.

And that's another thing about authentic happiness. It doesn't take away the reality of threat or risk or suffering; it's just there. This is one of the hardest things to get hold of here. How can I feel 'happy' in a world so full of atrocity and injustice? How can I know joy when I'm aware of my own failure, my own shabbiness, my own depression? There are no answers in theory because this isn't a matter of theory: it simply happens that way. People in the middle of extreme stress will witness to this. We might well remember today some of those in such situations – Christians facing threats and attacks in Pakistan or, right at the moment, in Northern Nigeria; and please pray and think of them, as some fanatics of all backgrounds seek to exploit religious differences there, even in the wake of what appears as a free and fair election. Or we might think of an aid worker in Congo, or a nurse or teacher in a strained and under-resourced institution, or a carer sitting through the night with a terminally ill child – people such as this will sometimes speak, shockingly, of feeling joy in the middle of what they endure. It is not – God forbid – feeling cheerful, it is not pretending that things aren't so bad after all. And it's a grim reproach that that's all too often what people half-expect from Christians, a glib and dishonest cheerfulness. No, it is an overwhelming sense of being where you should be, being in tune with something or someone, being rooted in the moment in a way that doesn't at all blur your honesty about what's there in front of your eyes but gives you what you need to sit in the presence of horror and grief, and live.

More than just a feeling, then, a passing emotion – certainly more than a self-conscious determination to put a brave face on things. Once again we have to be clear that it depends on something quite other than our efforts and our will power. And that takes us into a further dimension of joy. What we can contribute by our will or effort is not a system for making ourselves happy but a habit of readiness to receive. The person whose mind is completely cluttered with anxiety, self-absorbed worry or vanity or resentment is going to find it hard to give way to moments of gift and surprise. That's why people who are fairly used to taking time in silence and reflection may often be people in whom you see joy coming through. It's also why, for many of us, like the disciples at Easter, it takes something of a shock to open us up to joy, some experience that pushes its way through the inward clutter by sheer force and novelty. Perhaps part of the message of Easter is very simply, 'Be ready to be surprised; try clearing out some of the anxiety and vanity and resentment so as to allow the possibility of a new world to find room in you.'

But this means in turn that, rather than battling all the time to lay hold of a happiness that we have planned according to our fantasies, we should concentrate on challenging the things that make us anxious. About six weeks ago, I was visiting Manchester to see some of the work done by local churches and other faith groups for community regeneration; and I found myself listening more and more carefully for what these groups were saying about how the local people they worked with thought about well-being. They didn't have extravagant plans – but they simply identified a few conditions that would relieve loneliness, boredom and fear. Good and reliable mental health care, especially for the young; access to fresh air and space; opportunities to be creative, whether in growing vegetables or running a drama group. And it was impossible not to wonder where some of these hopes were on the scale of official priorities, in local or national government. On the same visit, an unscheduled stop at a local library in a rather devastated council estate revealed a lively group of teenagers who were regular users, welcomed by staff, glad of a place to do homework, gossip and feel secure. Space, opportunity, the time to discover a larger world to live in – where are the clearly articulated priorities in public discussion that would spotlight all this, so as to make us think twice before dismantling what's already there and disappointing more hopes for the future? Talk about the happiness of the nation isn't going to mean much unless we listen to some of these simple aspirations – aspirations, essentially, for places, provisions or situations which help you lay aside anxiety and discover dimensions of yourself otherwise hidden or buried.

Because, ultimately, joy is about discovering that the world is more than you ever suspected, and so that you yourself are more than you suspected. The joy of the resurrection has a unique place in

197

Christian faith and imagination because this event breaks open the shell of the world we thought we knew and projects us into the new and mysterious realm in which victorious mercy and inexhaustible love make the rules. And because it is the revelation of something utterly basic about reality itself, it is a joy that cannot just be at the mercy of passing feelings. It roots itself in the heart and remains as a foundation for everything else. The Christian is not therefore the person who has accepted a particular set of theories about the universe but the person who lives by the power of the joy that is laid bare in the event of the resurrection of Jesus. To be baptized 'into' Christ is to be given a lasting connection with joy, a channel through which the basic sense of being where we ought to be can always come through, however much we choke it up with selfishness and worry. Sometimes, clearing out this debris needs a bit of explosive – encounter with an extraordinary person or story, experience of passionate love, witnessing profound suffering, whatever shakes us out of our so-called 'normal' habits. But we can at least contribute to this by giving time to clearing the channel as best we may, in silence, in the space of reflection. And we can also ask persistently what it is in our social environment that will most help create this for others, especially those who live with constant anxiety because of poverty, disability or other sorts of disadvantage.

Christian joy, the joy of Easter, is offered to the world not to guarantee a permanently happy society in the sense of a society free from tension, pain or disappointment, but to affirm that whatever happens in the unpredictable world – sometimes wonderfully, sometimes horribly unpredictable – there is a deeper level of reality, a world within the world, where love and reconciliation are ceaselessly at work, a world with which contact can be made so that we are able to live honestly and courageously with the challenges constantly thrown at us. And on the first Easter morning, it is as if 'the fountains of the great deep' are broken open, and we are allowed to see, like Peter and John at the empty tomb, into the darkness for a moment – and find our world turned upside down, joy made possible.

BUT IS IT TRUE?

Easter 2012

It just might be the case that the high watermark of aggressive polemic against religious faith has been passed. Recent years have seen so many high-profile assaults on the alleged evils of religion that we've almost become used to them; we sigh and pass on, wishing that we could have a bit more of a sensible debate and a bit less hysteria. But there are a few signs that the climate is shifting ever so slightly – not towards a mass return to faith but at least towards a reluctant recognition that religion can't be blamed for everything – indeed that it has made and still makes positive contributions to our common life.

Two new books on the economic crisis, one by the American Michael Sandel, the other by Robert and Edward Skidelsky, both rather surprisingly float the idea that without some input from religious thinking our ludicrous and destructive economic habits are more likely to go unchecked. And, notoriously, Alain de Botton's recent book on how to hold on to the best bits of religion without the embarrassing beliefs that go with it created quite a public stir. If it doesn't exactly amount to a religious revival, it does suggest that a tide may be turning in how serious and liberal-minded commentators think about faith: no longer seen as a brainless and oppressive enemy, it is recognized as a potential ally in challenging a model of human activity and social existence that increasingly feels insane, a model in which unlimited material growth and individual acquisition still seem to trump every other argument about social coherence, international justice and realism in the face of limited resources. We may groan in spirit at the reports of how few young people in our country know the Lord's Prayer, but there is plenty to suggest that younger people, while still statistically deeply unlikely to be churchgoers, don't have the hostility to faith that one might expect, but at least share some of the Sandel–Skidelsky–de Botton sense that there is something here to take seriously – when they have a chance to learn about it. It is about the worst possible moment to downgrade the status and professional excellence of religious education in secondary schools – but that's another sermon.

So we have reason to feel thankful that things appear to be moving on from a pointless stalemate. Yet, granted all this, and given all the appropriate expression of relief Christians may allow themselves, Easter raises an extra question, uncomfortable and unavoidable: perhaps 'religion' *is* more useful than the passing generation of gurus thought; but is it *true?* Easter makes a claim not just about a potentially illuminating set of human activities but about an event in history and its relation to the action of God. Very simply, in the words of this morning's reading from the *Acts of the Apostles* (10.40), we are told that 'God raised Jesus to life'.

We are not told that Jesus 'survived death'; we are not told that the story of the empty tomb is a beautiful imaginative creation that offers inspiration to all sorts of people; we are not told that the message of Jesus lives on. We are told that God did something – that is, that this bit of the human record, the things that Peter and John and Mary Magdalene witnessed on Easter morning, is a moment when, to borrow an image from the twentieth-century Catholic writer Ronald Knox, the wall turns into a window. In this moment we see through to the ultimate energy behind and within all things. When the universe began, prompted by the will and act of God and maintained in being at every moment by the same will and action, God made it to be a universe in which on a particular Sunday morning in AD33 this will and action would come through the fabric of things and open up an unprecedented possibility – for Jesus and for all of us with him: the possibility of a human life together in which the pouring out of God's Holy Spirit makes possible a degree of reconciled love between us that could not have been imagined.

It is that reconciled love, and the whole picture of human destiny that goes with it, that attracts those outside the household of faith and even persuades them that the presence of religion in the social order may not be either toxic or irrelevant after all. But for the Christian, the basic fact is that this compelling vision is there only because God raised Jesus. It is not an idea conceived by the spiritual genius of the apostles, those horribly familiar characters with all their blundering and mediocrity, so like us. It is, as the gospel reading insists, a shocking novelty, something done for and to us, not by us. How do we know that it is true? Not by some final knock-down would-be scientific proof, but by the way it works in us through the long story of a whole life and the longer story of the life of the community that believes it. We learn and assimilate its truth by the risk of living it; to those on the edge of it, looking respectfully and wistfully at what it might offer, we can only say, 'You'll learn nothing more by looking; at some point you have to decide whether you want to try to live with it and in it.'

And what's the difference it makes? If God exists and is active, if his will and action truly raised Jesus from the dead, then what we think and do and achieve as human beings is not the only thing that the world's future depends on. We do all we can; we bring our best intelligence and energy to labour for reconciliation and for justice; but the future of reconciliation and justice doesn't depend only on us. To say this doesn't take away one jot of our responsibility or allow us to sit back; as Pascal said, we cannot sleep while Jesus is still in agony, and the continuing sufferings of the world are an image of that agony. But to believe that everything doesn't depend on us delivers us from two potentially deadly temptations. We may be tempted to do something, anything, just because we can't bear it if we aren't making some visible difference; but to act for the sake of acting is futile or worse. Or we

205

may be consumed with anxiety that we haven't done enough, so consumed that we never have time to be ourselves, to give God thanks for his love and grace and beauty. We may present a face to the world that is so frantic with fear that we have left something undone that we make justice and reconciliation deeply unattractive. We never acquire the grace and freedom to give God thanks for the small moments of joy, the little triumphs of sense and kindness.

And these things may be of real importance when we look at what seem to be the most completely intractable problems of our day. At Easter we cannot help but think about the land that Jesus knew and the city outside whose walls he was crucified. These last months have seen a phase of peace talks between Israel and the Palestinians yet again stalling, staggering and delivering little or nothing for those who most need signs of hope. Everything seems to be presented as a zero-sum game. And all who love both the Israeli and the Palestinian communities and long for their security will feel more desperate than ever. A visit to Yad Vashem, the Holocaust Museum in Jerusalem, will convince you why the state of Israel exists and must go on existing. A visit to

any border checkpoint will convince you that the
daily harassment and humiliation of Palestinians
of all ages and backgrounds cannot be a justi-
fiable or even sustainable price to pay for security.
Listening to a rabbi talking about what it is
like to witness the gathering up of body parts
after a terrorist attack is something that can't
be forgotten; neither is listening to a Palestinian
whose parent or child has been killed in front of
their eyes in a mortar bombing.

So how do we respond? By turning up the volume
of partisanship, by searching for new diplomatic
initiatives, by pretending it isn't as bad as all that
after all? If we believe in a God who acts, we have
to go beyond this. We have to put immense energy
into supporting those on the ground who show
that they believe in a God who acts – those who
continue, through networks like One Voice and
the Bereaved Families Forum, to bring together
people from both sides and challenge them to
discover empathy and mutual commitment –
what Stephen Cherry, in a wonderful book on
forgiveness, has called 'distasteful empathy', a
feeling for the other or the enemy that we would
rather not have to develop. Small moments of
recognition and kindness. We have to prod and

nag and encourage the religious leadership in
the Holy Land on all sides to speak as if they
believed in a God who acts, not only a God who
endorses their version of reality. We have to pray,
to pray for wisdom and strength and endurance
for all who are hungry for peace and justice, pray
that people will go on looking for a truly shared
future. And we Christians in particular have
to look for ways of practically supporting our
brothers and sisters there – through agencies like
the Friends of the Holy Land or the Jerusalem
and Middle East Church Association – to help
them stay in a context where they feel more and
more unwelcome, yet where they want to play
a full part in creating this unimaginable shared
future, because they believe in a God who acts.
These are the priorities that all Christian leaders
would want to flag up this Easter in our concern
for what many call 'the land of the Holy One'.

One situation among many – but how can it
not be on our minds and hearts at this time of
the Christian year, this central moment of hope?
Such situations can so readily draw us towards
despair, including the despair of hyper-activism
and unfocused anger. To believe in a God who
raises Jesus from the dead is never an alibi, letting

us do less than we thought we would have to. But it is a way of allowing in our own thoughts and actions some space for God to emerge as a God who creates a future. Someone once remarked that resurrection was never something you could plan for. But what we can do is to make the space, the silence, for the act of God to come through. When all's said and done about the newly acknowledged social value of religion, we mustn't forget that what we ultimately have to speak about isn't this but God: the God who raised Jesus and, as St Paul repeatedly says, will raise us also with him. Even if every commentator in the country expressed generous appreciation of the Church (and we probably needn't hold our breath ...), we'd still be bound to say 'Thank you – but what matters isn't our usefulness or niceness or whatever: it's God, purposive and active, even – especially – when we are at the end of our resources. It's the moment when the wall becomes a window.'